A CRY IN THE WILDERNESS

A CRY IN THE WILDERNESS

Twelve bold messages about uncompromising faith

KEITH GREEN

Introduction by Melody Green Sievright
Edited by David Hazard, and Geoff and Janet Benge

SPARROW

Sparrow Press
Nashville, Tennessee

Published 1993 in Nashville, Tennessee, by Sparrow Press, and distributed in Canada by Christian Marketing Canada, Ltd.

Printed in the United States of America

97 96 95 94 93   5 4 3 2 1

Library of Congress Cataloging-in-Publication Data

Green, Keith, 1953-1982
    A cry in the wilderness : twelve bold messages about uncompromising faith / Keith Green : introduction by Melody Green Sievright.
        p.   cm.
    ISBN 0-917143-14-0 : $12.95
    1. Christian life- - 1960 -   I. Title.
BV4501.2. G74515   1993
248.4- -dc20
                                    93-88
                                    CIP

Unless otherwise noted, Scripture taken from the New American Standard Bible, © 1960, 1962, 1963, 1968, 1971, 1972, 1973, 1975, 1977 by The Lockman Foundation. Used by permission.

Grateful acknowledgement is made for permission to quote from: *Rees Howells, Intercessor* by Norman Grubb. © 1967 by Christian Literature Crusade.

Quotes featured in each chapter are from the following:
Ch. 1: Oswald Chambers, *My Utmost for His Highest.* Ch. 2: Charles Finney, *Lectures On Revival.* Ch. 3: Andrew Murray, *Coming Revival.* Ch. 4: Francis Schaeffer, *True Spirituality.* Ch. 5: C. S. Lewis, *The Four Loves.* Ch. 6: Rees Howells in Norman Grubb, *Rees Howells, Intercessor.* Ch. 7: Amy Carmichael, *Candles in the Dark.* Ch. 8: John Wesley, *Messages on the Sermon on the Mount.* Ch. 9: Oswald Chambers, *My Utmost for His Highest.* Ch. 10: Hannah Hurnard, *Hind's Feet on High Places.* Ch. 11: William Booth in Richard Collier, *The General Next to God.* Ch. 12: Charles Finney, *Lectures on Revival.*

Design by Garrett Rittenberry

CONTENTS

INTRODUCTION

In the days before Jesus walked the earth, God's people always seemed to be surrounded by a conquering enemy. Even after the birth of Jesus, the enemy often appeared to be in charge. Roman soldiers armed to the teeth roamed the highways and swaggered arrogantly down the city streets. The power was in the hands of those who opposed all that God, and those who loved Him, stood for.

It was during this time that God sent a voice with an important announcement. This voice emerged from nowhere in a camel's hair tunic and cried out, "Make way for the Lord!" The voice was strong and determined. And like the cry of a hungry baby in the middle of the night, it refused to be ignored. It drew followers and critics alike.

It also drew fire.

To silence that voice, the head of an innocent young man was crudely separated from his body. That day a line was drawn in the desert sand. The stakes got higher for everyone who considered becoming a disciple of Jesus Christ—the One that John the Baptist proclaimed.

It was not easy to follow Jesus in those days.

Even though things have changed significantly today, Christians are still in a similar position. We're surrounded by people who resist God and oppose His truth. They make up their own rules and not only live out, but sometimes legislate, their own ideas of morality and justice. We see these ideas everywhere we look—in the media, music and arts, films and politics. We are bombarded with messages that openly mock our faith and our values.

Today, most of us aren't surrounded by a literal enemy army, but the attack often comes when the subtle gray fog of enemy "logic" is blown over the absolutes of the gospel. The enemy knows that if he can cloud the lines between God's holy standard and his ungodly schemes, people will become confused and double minded.

It's no wonder we hear such schizophrenic reasoning as the world pumps out mixed messages in compelling packages. They warn us not to use drugs or abuse alcohol, then glorify addictive lifestyles. They caution against casual sex because of sexually transmitted diseases, then belittle chastity and faithfulness in marriage. They spend a fortune lobbying to protect animals and trees, but demand the right to kill unborn babies.

Even the most spiritually dull should be able to see that something is terribly wrong with the "logic" of worldly thinking. We can't afford to be vague and unsure about what is black and white in God's sight. That's why we must know God's heart—so we can hold His standards high.

If our thinking is not aligned in any area with God's truth, our lives won't be aligned either. Our foundation in the Lord must be strong enough to withstand the gray fog that blows our way every day. We not only need to know what we believe, but why we believe it. Thankfully, God has raised up determined voices in our generation. These voices challenge us to examine our hearts. They ask us if what we believe in our minds is actually being lived out in our lives. They sober us as they cry out, "Get your life in order. Jesus is going to come again and you'd better get ready!"

Keith Green was one of those voices.

He was strong, persistent, hard to ignore. He spoke the truth we needed to hear then, and perhaps like never before, need to hear now. In the seven brief years that Keith knew Jesus he trumpeted a wake-up call to Christians everywhere. "It's time to quit playing church and start *being* the Church," Keith said.

Keith was my husband for almost nine years and I watched him struggle to live the truth without compromise. In the process he identified the struggles each of us face. How do we physically live in one world we're told not to be part of—and at the same time totally give our hearts to a realm we can't see with our eyes or touch with our hands? And when the world tells us to compromise—in all too compelling ways—how do we maintain our fire, our integrity and our purity?

In the days of John the Baptist some of the darkness was easier to detect. Multitudes openly practiced witchcraft, worshipped demonic idols and participated in religious rituals with temple prostitutes. Meanwhile, Roman soldiers swore allegiance to the false god, Caesar, and stood in murderous opposition to God's people. The same dark spirits that were loose then are still running rampant. But now their schemes are often cloaked with greater subtlety to appeal to our more "civilized" senses. Today we're too sophisticated to lop off someone's head. But in some ways it's worse.

The biggest question Keith tried to answer in his life and in his teachings was one we all ask: What does it mean to be a true disciple of Jesus Christ?

Perhaps more than many of his contemporaries, Keith recognized the powerful truth that we cannot serve two masters. "We can't serve Jesus and the world at the same time," Keith said. "Jesus is coming back for a spotless Bride. What bridegroom would marry someone who was messin' around with someone else on the side?"

Keith Green held up an often uncomfortable standard. He was certain of the Biblical premise that we're either hot or cold—that if we don't sell out to Jesus we're certain to sell out to the world. This is the reality for all of us. How do we become more captive to Christ? Can we give ourselves to Him in greater ways? How do we develop discernment that safeguards us and those we love? How can we receive more of God's presence and grace in our lives each day?

Most Christians I know want to keep growing in the Lord. It's a constant challenge, but we can have victory if we understand God's character and stubbornly stick to His principles. Keith understood how difficult being a disciple of Jesus is when we're surrounded by such spiritual darkness. That's why I believe this book is so timely today.

In a season when so many Christians are tempted to climb over the fence to "greener pastures," Keith's teachings sound a warning to point the way home. Perhaps it's time for all of us, young and old in the Lord, to take a long, honest look at where we're at with God—and where we want to be. It's never too late, this side of eternity, to fix any cracks we might find in our foundation.

Keith and I became Christians in 1975, and his musical talent propelled him to the top of the music charts in a few short years. He is most remembered for the powerful soul-searching songs he wrote and sang. Those songs, coupled with Keith's passionate and powerful delivery, are still changing lives around the world today.

But in spite of the legacy of music Keith left behind, all that he had to say was not fully captured in his musical recordings. How could it be? He had a keen intellect and an intense desire to see God honored across the face of the earth—and he didn't mind talking about his convictions.

Keith's spiritual foundation was influenced strongly by reading the works of great Christians who loved God's people and the Church—even as they labored to ignite them with greater passion for God. Men like Charles Finney, Oswald Chambers, Francis Schaeffer, William Booth and Rees Howells helped form Keith's spiritual understanding, as did women like Amy Carmichael and Hannah Hurnard. Their writings formed a rock-solid platform of conviction in him, second only to his love for the Word of God. If you ever attended one of Keith's concerts or Bible studies, you knew he was willing to stand for God's truth whether people agreed with him or not. He was also willing to be misunderstood or suffer rejection for his convictions. To him truth was timeless, and it did not matter if others called him controversial. Keith would say, "I've never *tried* to be controversial. The truth is controversial enough!"

Of course, it is important to speak the truth in love—and I'm sure there are times we could be a lot better at it—but if we stop speaking the truth at all, then we'll begin to live compromised lives. It is imperative that our lives be marked by love and compassion, but we can't replace being people who please the Lord with being people pleasers. Obviously, the dividing line can be difficult to discern at times. That's why we need to keep our hearts turned towards the Lord, trusting the Holy Spirit to show us if we've crossed over any lines.

By his own admission there were times Keith could have seasoned his preaching with a bit more grace. But the overall content of his message has shaken hundreds of thousands of Christians into a more reverent, holy, all-out devotion to Jesus Christ. There has been, and continues to be, good fruit from his life and ministry.

Besides his message to Christians, Keith also was a compelling evangelist. He was always open to "divine appointments" with strangers. Keith not only led people to the Lord by the thousands at his concerts, but one by one in restaurants, at the beach, in the woods and even in our living room. Often these new believers had nowhere to go, so we took them into our home.

In a short time, our little three-bedroom house in Southern California was bursting at the seams. With money earned from Keith's concerts and our songwriter's salary from CBS Records, we bought a second house and rented five other homes in our neighborhood to give young believers a place to grow in Christ. Soon our community had about seventy new Christians living in one of our seven homes—unwed moms, bikers, ex-junkies and lots of young seekers who had given up on eastern mysticism for the truth of Jesus Christ. They were all hungry and needed to be fed—physically and spiritually.

One of Keith's favorite things was teaching—and he often taught several nights a week. Keith would sit on the living room floor cross-legged and barefoot, open his Bible, and begin to preach like there was no tomorrow. He was spurred on by the sea of eager faces before him, hungry to learn about God. Most had little or no understanding about what it meant to follow Jesus—and it was Keith's great joy to tell them. Friends from church and even some neighbors began to fill our living room for Keith's studies.

We continued to grow and in 1977 we legally incorporated as a non-profit ministry and officially became Last Days Ministries—or LDM. Then in 1979, we moved to a 140-acre ranch in the gentle green hills of East Texas with lots of room to expand. Once in Texas, Keith continued to teach regularly. His teachings were always powerful yet practical as he opened the Word to us with humor, insight and wisdom often beyond his years. Keith taught us about living a life that was 100 percent sold-out to God, about counting the cost, picking up our cross, prayer, suffering and about giving God total lordship over our lives.

Keith delivered some of the best Bible studies I've ever heard—literally hundreds of them. That's where this book came from. We transcribed, edited and organized a virtual mountain of Keith's teaching tapes, picking for this book the ones we felt best spoke to the issues we face today. You may be surprised to see that in addition to Keith's world-renowned music ministry, he left behind such a vast legacy of excellent teaching.

Interestingly, there are Christians now with the Lord, like Oswald Chambers and Peter Marshall, whose words were never published in their lifetime. And just as their teachings have enriched so many lives through the years, it is my prayer that this book of Keith's teachings will do the same. That's why we've taken great care to preserve the integrity of Keith's message—which seems more relevant today than ever.

Through the course of our marriage and ministry together Keith's teachings affected me in an eternal way. I was there when he taught most of the Bible studies reflected in this book, and listening to him laid a strong Biblical foundation in my life.

Today, more than ever, I see how Keith's teachings helped prepare me for what I faced when the Lord took him home in 1982 along with two of our children—Josiah, who was three, and Bethany, who was two—and nine other dear friends. From the first moment of the airplane crash God carried me through the most devastating time of my life. I'm grateful that Keith's ministry gave me insight about God's faithfulness and sovereignty. If I hadn't understood that sometimes Christians suffer for reasons we don't comprehend, I wonder if my faith would have remained intact after such a tragedy.

Little did I know that Keith's life would help prepare me for his death.

Keith's teachings will help lay a solid foundation in your life, too. Because they are born of the Spirit, they are timeless. In fact, at Last Days Ministries we're always receiving requests for his music and teaching from

Christians who have "discovered" Keith for the first time.

Whether you're a new Christian or mature in your faith, this book will challenge and strengthen you. There are certain foundational stones every Christian needs to have in place for the long-term fruitfulness and stability of his or her spiritual life. That's what this book is about. Although I've been a Christian for eighteen years, reading the material in this book challenged me again in a powerful way.

Periodically, each of us needs to take a fresh look at our lives to be sure our foundation doesn't have any cracks. In the physical realm, builders erect a structure based on the size of the foundation. A building can't be bigger than its foundation—and it can only be as tall as the foundation is deep. Too often we think God has erected a large structure in our lives, but in reality we lack the power and vitality in Christ we know we should have.

In the spiritual realm, God only allows us to have as much of Him as our foundation, or life in Him, will support. If we want a powerful ministry that is Spirit-anointed, our house must be built upon the Rock. So when the storms come (and they will) our house will stand.

In the past several years the Church has heard wonderful teachings on every subject imaginable. We've learned important principles on aspects of the kingdom that have enriched our lives. But when we assess our lives we can't afford to say, "Well, my family is in order, my finances are man-aged biblically, I know how to do spiritual warfare—I guess I'm doing just fine!" These are all very good things, but we can't let the principles of the Lord—no matter how important they are—replace our relationship with Him.

Keith's message is significant today because God is calling us back to Him in a fresh way. The Lord wants us to check out our foundations and see if any cracks need to be repaired. And now is the time to do it. Why? Because God is preparing to pour out His Spirit across the earth. He will begin showing up in ways we've only dreamed about—and He wants each of us to be ready to play an important part with Him when it happens. Someone once said, "The future belongs to those who are prepared for it." If we want to be a part of the next powerful move of God, we need to get ready now.

At this moment, the Lord is preparing us to be the kind of "contain-ers" that can receive every bit of Him—and His power—we can possibly hold. But first we need to empty our lives of anything that hinders us from being filled with Him in a fresh way. If the absolutes of the Lord have become shrouded by the gray fog of enemy "logic," we need the breath of the Holy Spirit to blow it away. Maybe some of the world has rubbed off on us, or perhaps compromise has gained some ground in our life. If so, we need to take back the land! Then we can go out in God's anointing and strength to change our world with His love, for His glory.

Today the Lord continues to speak to us through the passionately intense voice of Keith Green. Keith challenged us to love God with our whole hearts. He had a burning desire to see the Lord honored with all we have, all we say and all we do. With the grace and power of God we can gain the victory we need. The Lord wants each of us to fulfill the destiny He has for us. He wants to use us in mighty ways for His glory in this important generation.

Whether you're young or old, married or single, my prayer for you as you read this book is that your passion for the Lord be ignited in a fresh way—that you will love Him like never before and be filled to overflowing with His power and light. God wants you to be hungry for His presence and to love His Holy Spirit. It's time for any grayness or confusion that may have crept into your life to be detected and dispelled so you can move forward in God's strength.

I also pray that this book will help you find your own voice, and that when you do, you'll speak boldly as the Lord leads you—whether it's over a cup of coffee, or like Keith, in a voice that's heard around the world.

Melody Green Sievright
April 1993

Jesus said,

"Rightly did Isaiah
prophesy of you . . .
   as it is written,
      'This people honors Me
   with their lips,
         but their heart
   is far away from Me…
      teaching as doctrines
   the precepts of men.'"

                              Mark 7:6-7

Follow
The Right Gospel

Yet [God] has now reconciled you in His fleshly body through death, in order to present you before Him holy and blameless and beyond reproach—if indeed you continue in the faith firmly established and steadfast, and not moved away from the hope of the gospel that you have heard, which was proclaimed in all creation under heaven, and of which I, Paul, was made a minister (Colossians 1:22-23).

◆

The Apostle Paul warns us about other gospels that may entice us away from the true gospel. Paul is very blunt about this in his letter to the Galatians:

> I am amazed that you are so quickly deserting Him who called you by the grace of Christ, for a *different gospel;* which is really not another; only there are some who are disturbing you, and want to distort the gospel of Christ (Galatians 1:6-7, emphasis added).

Are you following the true gospel—the one Jesus preached? The one Paul and the other apostles preached? How do you know? What are the consequences if you are not following the right gospel?

The word *gospel* means "good news." Even in Paul's day, other preachers had different types of "good news" for their listeners. Some preached that salvation could be obtained through eating the right foods. Others said you had to join the Jewish religion or practice strict personal disciplines in order to be saved. There was the Gnostic gospel, which was a type of early mysticism, and the reformed Jewish gospel and all kinds of other gospels. There were even other so-called "messiahs" around at the time of Christ.

Things haven't changed much, have they?

Most born-again Christians can see through heretical teachings. Some of those teachings are so far off the wall it's hard to believe anyone could take them seriously. But other false teachings are much more subtle and difficult to spot—especially when they infiltrate the *true gospel*. The teachers of these other gospels try to convince us that things are not as black and white as Paul makes them out to be. They tell us that there is a little room to accommodate the flesh—to expect wealth and good health. Or that the way pointed out in the Bible is just an *ideal*—goals we're meant to aim at but not expected to hit. All these ideas are designed to appeal to our flesh, and Satan uses them to lull us until we're ineffective.

But the gospel that Paul preached involved making tough choices and taking hard stands. It was about putting your life on the line. Losing popularity with your friends. Suffering for your convictions. Paul himself lived through all these challenges. After his encounter with Christ on the road to Damascus, he became a wanted man, hunted down by the same Pharisees who had been his friends and colleagues. Why? Because he spoke against their "gospels"—which were no gospels at all. They were just vain attempts to offer God religious practices He wasn't really interested in. What God wants is *all* of us—heart, soul, mind and body.

So, Paul was imprisoned for his beliefs. He suffered torture and beatings. And from this vantage point he urged both Timothy and the Galatians to be wary of a gospel that's more comfortable. A gospel that allows you to withhold your heart from God and offer him a few trinkets. Through the things he endured in his life, Paul showed that he had the credentials to speak and teach with authority about the true gospel.

What was the true gospel for which Paul gave up everything? Here's what he told Timothy:

> [God's grace] has been revealed by the appearing of our Savior Christ Jesus, who abolished death, and brought life and immortality to light through the gospel, for which I was appointed a preacher and an apostle and a teacher. For this reason I also suffer these things, but I am not ashamed; for I

know whom I have believed and I am convinced that He is able to guard what I have entrusted to Him until that day. Retain the standard of sound words which you have heard from me, in the faith and love which are in Christ Jesus. Guard, through the Holy Spirit who dwells in us, the treasure which has been entrusted to you (2 Timothy 1:10-14).

I want to warn you about this: There are a lot of "other gospels." Most of them appeal to our flesh. They avoid challenge and sacrifice. But they are not the true gospel that leads us to salvation. One mark of the true gospel is that it demands sacrifice from us. Sacrifice of having control of our lives, moment by moment. It challenges everything we do. But as we learn to embrace the gospel—and to realize that this world is not our final home—and when we live it out in our lives, God will use us to call the world to himself.

If anyone exemplified a changed life, it was Rees Howells, a famous preacher and a leader in the great Welsh Revival in the early 1900s. He went on to be used by God to bring revival to England, Ireland and Africa. Howells insisted that his effectiveness for Christ came from one incident when he was twenty-seven years old—he had a life-changing encounter with the Holy Spirit. This is how Norman Grubb describes it in Howells' biography:

> The meeting with the Holy Ghost was just as real to [Howells] as his [conversion to Christianity] three years before. "I saw him as a person apart from flesh and blood and He said to me, 'As the Savior had a body, so I dwell in the cleansed temple of the believer. I am God and I come to ask you to give your body to me, that I may work through you. I need a body for my temple.
>
> 'But it must belong to me without reserve for two persons with different wills can never live in the same body. Will you give me yours?
>
> 'You must go out. I shall not mix myself with yourself.' I saw the honor He gave me in offering to indwell me but there were many things very dear to me and I knew He wouldn't keep even one of them. The change He would make was very clear. It meant every bit of my fallen nature was to

go to the cross and He would bring His own life and His own nature into me. It was unconditional surrender."[1]

The story continues with God giving Howells an ultimatum: Would he obey or not? He had to give God his reply the following week.

For the next few days Howells wept continually. He couldn't eat or sleep and he lost seven pounds. This was the hardest decision he would ever have to make—to hand over his life like a blank check to God. Was he willing to let go of all his dreams, all his possessions, and let the Holy Spirit take full control?

This is what happened when he reached his decision:

> "Nothing was more real to me than the process I went through for that whole week....The Holy Spirit went on dealing with me exposing the root of my nature which was self and you can only get out of a thing what is in its root. Sin was cancelled and it wasn't sin He was dealing with; it was *self*—that thing which came from the Fall. He was not going to take any superficial surrender. He put His finger on each part of my self-life, and I have to decide in cold-blood. He could never take a thing away until I gave my consent."[2]

Like the Apostle Paul, Howells found God does not want us to play games. There comes a time when the Holy Spirit puts His finger on areas in our life and asks us to hand over control of them to Him. In order to receive the resurrection life and the power that goes along with it, we must be willing to let go of everything we hold close. Sometimes our flesh screams as we do this. Other times it devises subtle ways of getting us off-track. Instead of kicking and screaming, our flesh quietly tries to distract us with side issues—anything to keep us from giving everything to God. Suddenly, small matters of theology become major issues as we focus on anything but what the Holy Spirit wants to deal with.

Have you ever noticed how easily small children can be distracted? Give children candy, and you can walk off with all their toys. For awhile, they'll be so happy with the candy they won't even notice.

Believers can be like that too. Paul continually reminded the Christians of his day to stay on-track. If they did not stay focused on Christ, the Way, other preachers would come along to lead them astray with their fleshly gospels. Some people focused on getting rich quick, like Simon the sorcerer (Acts 8:9-25). Others sought to turn the gospel into a purely mystical experience. And still others wanted to bog down the whole message in Jewish laws and customs. After about two months, if these young Christians hadn't received a letter from Paul, they would begin to listen to these other gospels. They wanted to see if other interpretations of the Christian life were easier to follow. Though they were hungry for spiritual truth, their flesh kept tempting them to believe many things that weren't the gospel of the kingdom.

———————— ◆ ————————

Today Jesus Christ is being despatched as the Figurehead of a Religion, a mere example. He is that, but He is infinitely more; He is salvation itself, He is the Gospel of God.
— Oswald Chambers

———————— ◆ ————————

I once heard a prophecy that the city of Chicago was going to be leveled by an earthquake on a particular day. I thought, *I'll believe it when I see it.* A couple of young Christians I worked with got excited. "What time will it hit?" one of them asked me. He was so trusting. Another one said, "I have an uncle in Chicago. I'm going to call him and tell him to get out before it's too late." I can understand their concern, because there was a time when I would have been swayed by the gospel of sensationalism. I used to look for big signs to occur too. As a result I was easily led astray. I believed things that were not doctrinally sound.

Here's the point: Each one of us must take responsibility before God to keep our eyes on the gospel. We can't allow anything or anyone to distract or mislead us.

Paul gave some strong warnings about this:

> Even though we, or an angel from heaven, should preach to you a gospel contrary to that which we have preached to you, *let him be accursed.* As we have said before, so I say again now,

if any man is preaching to you a gospel contrary to that which you received, let him be accursed. For am I now seeking the favor of men, or of God? Or am I striving to please men? If I were still trying to please men, I would not be a bond-servant of Christ (Galatians 1:8-10, emphasis added).

How can we know for sure that we're following the true gospel? Paul laid out for Timothy the hallmarks of the person who has embraced the true gospel. We need to see if these things are part of our lives.

Here's the first:

It is a trustworthy statement: For if we died with Him, we shall also live with Him (2 Timothy 2:11).

The heart of the gospel is that we must die with Christ in order to live with Him. But what exactly does it mean to die with Christ? To begin, it means that we are to be dead to our rights. And that means signing over to God our desires, our dreams, our hurts. All that we are or will be.

What do you think Paul meant when he said, "For you have died and your life is hidden with Christ in God" (Colossians 3:3)? He wasn't talking about a theory, or a nice metaphor. He meant that at the point of real salvation we are nailed to the cross with Jesus. We go down to the grave. And a new life—God's life—is born in us.

What we're talking about, at the deepest level, is an exchange of our will. I give my will over to God, and begin to pursue His will for me.

A lot of people get stuck on certain behaviors—old habits, for instance. They want to clean up their flesh without becoming pure in heart first. You become pure in heart by wanting what God wants. It's easy to give up your wrongs—but much harder to give up your rights. Have you ever heard of a dead person calling a lawyer from the grave to sue someone for violating his rights? The dead have no rights.

What about me, as a Christian? I have no rights. I have no right to run a ministry. I have no right to own a car. But in Christ, I do have a right to inherit all of God's promises in the Bible—if I can prove to myself, to the world and to Jesus that I am dead. Here's a promise our flesh might not like to claim: "If we have died with Him, we will be raised with Him." The "if" is a crucial part. People who follow the wrong gospel want to make the "ifs" invisible. They like to think there are no conditions in the Bible. True, God's love is not conditional—but there is a condition on experiencing the true life of Christ. It is giving over my will. That means I have stopped manipulating God's Word for my own gain.

Have you died with Christ? Or are you trying to live with Him at the same time you're doing everything to accommodate your own fleshly desires?

Like Rees Howells, God requires each of us to make a choice. You cannot have your life and the life of Christ residing in you at the same time. The Holy Spirit doesn't want the flesh for a roommate.

The problem for most of us is that we want a spiritual crown, yet we want to avoid the cross that must come first. But as Paul says:

> *If* we endure, we shall also reign with Him (2 Timothy 2:12, emphasis added).

When people read this they think, *Yes! I'm going to reign with Christ.* They ignore the "if." They think God is going to endure *for* them. So they sit back and act as if God will do all the work.

The problem is, Paul turned the spotlight on us: *We* are to endure. How do we do it? We endure by casting everything—hopes and cares alike—upon Him. That's our work of faith: to identify every fleshly goal or care that draws us away from God, and cast it all over to Him. Dying to it. Faith is not just a hope—faith is a deed. It's active, not passive. Faith is God and me in partnership. First, His will replaces mine, then His power enables me to do all that He says.

"If we endure...," Paul says. And we endure by entering into the will of God. It's when we do His will that God blesses us. We can't be blessed in a place where His will does not reign.

If we're going to endure—to choose the high road of faith—then we have to be prepared for some attacks. We might as well know this from the start. Be prepared. Count the cost. So we don't get weary and give up.

First, we'll have to endure assaults on our soul by the devil. Peter says,

> Be of sober spirit, be on the alert. Your adversary, the devil, prowls about like a roaring lion, seeking someone to devour. But resist him, firm in your faith, knowing that the same

experiences of suffering are being accomplished by your brethren who are in the world (1 Peter 5:8-9).

Satan is the most powerful being in the universe, apart from God. He's like a lion on the prowl, looking for unsuspecting Christians to chew up. He's inflamed with pride, jealousy, greed and with the power God has allowed him to keep. Our conflict is not against flesh and blood, but against the rulers of the darkness of this world. And to fight them, we need spiritual weapons—truth, salvation and prayer (Ephesians 6:10-20). When we choose God's will, we're guaranteed the power of the Holy Spirit in order to endure the assaults of the devil.

Second, we must endure false teachings, holding on to the truth even when it is not popular. In Hebrews we read,

Jesus Christ is the same yesterday and today, yes and forever. Do not be carried away by varied and strange teachings (Hebrews 13:8-9).

When Melody and I were new Christians, all sorts of people came to our Bible studies. I'll never forget one guy in particular. He was a new believer, but he came with every spiritual book imaginable—including a Bible, a concordance and an "Aquarian Gospel of Jesus Christ." I'd begin a Bible study, and he'd take over, reading from all these other spiritual books. He spent hours telling us that eating meat was of the devil. He went on and on about weird doctrines.

I lost touch with him for a long time, and then I saw him at a convention. He told me he'd just come back from Israel where he chanted on the streets. As I listened to his experiences I thought, *Here's a brand-new believer who never got off the ground!* He couldn't discern false teaching and he wouldn't listen to anyone who might help him. He was completely derailed. All kinds of seeds of darkness had been sown in him and he had no way to fend them off.

In the end times we're going to experience false teachings that are doctrines of demons, and smooth-sounding teachings that are really antichrist. There will be people close to becoming Christians, but who nevertheless are deceived. Do we have a safeguard? Yes, by listening only to teachers in whose lives we can see the fruit of the Spirit—those who *do* what they *preach.*

Finally, we know we're following the right gospel if we learn to endure and overcome the lusts of the flesh—and by that, I mean, we're learning to live free from all the things that seek to bind us to this world. John warned us against "the lust of the eyes and the pride of life" (1 John 2:16). And Paul warned us to flee from immorality (1 Corinthians 6:18), and to pursue righteousness (2 Timothy 2:22). A lot of Christians know how to flee—they get out of the world—but they don't know how to pursue righteousness—that is, they don't know how to get the world out of them.

Paul told us to "set our affections on things above" (Colossians 3:2). Not only are we supposed to be turning away *from* something, we're supposed to be turning ourselves—heart, soul, body and mind—*toward* something. Toward the "prize of the high calling" to be like Jesus in this world (Philippians 3:14). What is that high calling? Like Paul, I want to be found growing in the image and likeness of Jesus Christ when God calls me home or when Jesus comes back, whichever comes first. I want to be a true disciple —one who has set his affections on the wonderful things that are above. That means letting go of all that this world offers by way of security and honor and pleasure.

And that's how we'll know if we are following the true gospel. The true gospel challenges us at every turn. It unsettles us. It requires things of us that hurt. Our flesh will squirm. The devil will attack us in our weakest areas. Other Christians will offer us less radical ways to follow Christ. But in the end, we'll be transformed from the inside out. We'll be clean. We'll be shining lights.

And then everything we say will be light and grace to people lost in this dark wilderness in which we live. Then we'll know by the fruit of the Spirit in our lives that we are His disciples.

Notes
1. Norman Grubb, *Rees Howells, Intercessor* (Fort Washington, Penn.: Christian Literature Crusade, 1967) 38-40.
2. Ibid

John the Baptist said,

" …every tree

that does not bear

good fruit

is cut down

and thrown

into the fire."

Matthew 3:10

Produce
The Fruit Of Repentance

Therefore leaving the elementary teaching about the Christ, let us press on to maturity, not laying again a foundation of repentance from dead works and of faith toward God (Hebrews 6:1, emphasis added).

———————◆———————

Charles Finney was a leader in the great revival that swept through America during the nineteenth century. Even though he was considered radical by some, we need to take a look at his ministry—because he set his world on fire with the gospel.

When Finney came into a town, he held what he called an "anxious inquirer's meeting" for people who were worried about the state of their souls. At these meetings Finney didn't preach. He simply told people that in order to receive salvation they needed to repent and be forgiven. Then he'd quietly exit the room and leave the people alone with God. No manipulating. No emotional pitch. No pressure.

What happened? God's Spirit dealt with people, and they came under tremendous conviction of sin. People wept as they begged God to have mercy on them. You'd think a revivalist preacher would jump on this, wouldn't you? But Finney wouldn't lead them in the sinner's prayer—he'd send them home for the night instead. Why? Because he didn't want false conversions. He believed that sinners needed to be so deeply convicted of their sin by the Holy Spirit that they turned from their old lives to pursue God with every ounce of strength.

How effective was Finney's approach? The fact is, few of the many thousands who came to the Lord under his ministry ever backslid.

It's time for us to learn what Finney knew about conversion.

First of all, he understood the role of the Holy Spirit in bringing a person to repentance and new life in Christ. He let the Holy Spirit do His work in the hearts of people. Finney was careful not to rob the Holy Spirit of His role by bringing people to premature conversions.

How different things are today. When *only* one-fourth of the people who come to the Lord through a given ministry go on with God and don't backslide, we think that's success. Finney would shudder.

Why are things this way? Why is it that people give up the Christian life after putting their hands to the plow? Why is it that we settle for so much less in our spiritual lives—less power, less love, less fruit?

One reason is that we've made the message of salvation too easy. Repentance is the condition for salvation—but we neglect to talk about it. It has become an option not a requirement.

I can't find one place in Scripture where God offers forgiveness before repentance. His offer is always the same, whether it's to the Jews or to Christians in the early church: "If you repent of your sin, you will be forgiven."

This is what Jesus said to a crowd of religious leaders and common people alike: "I tell you…unless you repent, you will all likewise perish" (Luke 13:3). That's pretty sobering.

Jesus' disciples preached the same message: "And they went out and preached that men should repent" (Mark 6:12).

When Peter stood to preach on the day of Pentecost, what was his message? "Repent, and let each of you be baptized in the name of Jesus Christ for the forgiveness of your sins…" (Acts 2:38).

What about Paul? He said, "[I] kept declaring both to those of Damascus first, and also at Jerusalem and then throughout all the region of Judea, and even to the Gentiles, that they should repent and turn to God, performing deeds appropriate to repentance" (Acts 26:20).

Stop and consider this a moment. If we're honest, we have to admit that today's preaching seems a long way from the message the early disciples taught. A lot of preachers today sound more like used car salespersons than ministers of the gospel. It's as if they're selling Christianity as the "ultimate ride." "Do you want to be rid of all your worries? Do you want to have joy? Peace? Do you want to get rid of all the problems in your life? Then step right up and receive Jesus. Say yes to Him…"

And the sinner who's listening says, "Yeah, I want all that. I want joy and peace. I want to know I'm going to heaven. I want to feel like I did when I won the trip to Hawaii. And all I've got to do is say yes. It's the deal of the century!"

So people run forward to answer altar calls. Someone leads them in a "sinner's prayer"—which you can't find anywhere in Scripture. Then they're handed a Bible and told to read it once a day, and pray. They get a pat on the back. And someone says, "Praise the Lord! You're born-again. You're a Christian now!"

But did that man or woman ever hear about *repentance*? Not too often. We seem more interested in signatures on a decision card than in making sure a person has met all the conditions for receiving forgiveness and for growing into a child of God.

What happens? These people go home and for the first few days everything is great. They feel joyful and happy—just like when they won the trip to Hawaii. They read their Bible and pray, just like they were told. Then things start coming apart. Their boss gets mad at them. Their car gets scratched. Their dog gets run over. Their investments don't pay off. Their old friends drop them. Pretty soon they're back where they started. They say, "Where is all this peace I was promised? Where's the blessing? God isn't real." Then they may turn their backs and walk away, because they didn't find the easy, happy life they were looking for. Why? Because we failed to tell them that the ultimate goal of accepting Christ is not to be happy every minute of the day.

I'm not for going around with long faces. But let's face it, the Bible isn't filled with stories of God making people happy. It's filled with stories of Him making people *holy*. And there's a long process involved in making people holy. It takes time. It isn't comfortable. Sometimes it downright hurts. But if we're patient and cooperate with God, we will reap the benefits of His working in our lives. We may not always know happiness, but we can have His peace throughout the process.

So what was it that Jesus meant—and Peter, Paul and the rest of the disciples—when they talked about repentance?

First, they meant something more than feeling sorry for our sins. I think most sinners are sorry for their sins. I took drugs for three years and I was sorry the whole time—sorry about what I was doing to myself, sorry that I was caught in a trap. But being sorry never got me out of the snare of drugs. Prisoners are sorry, too—sorry they're in prison! Prison ministers will tell you a lot of inmates say, "I'm sorry about the state my life's in.

When I get out of here, I'm going straight." But feeling sorry isn't enough to turn a person's life around. The next time they get caught and end up back in jail, they'll be sorry again. So, if repentance means *feeling* sorry about our sin, then like Charles Finney said, hell is filled with repentant people.

But repentance means *changing the way we think about God and about sin*. It means realigning our feelings and actions. Choosing to hate sin and love God. Seeing the pain and destruction our sin has brought to God, to other people and to ourselves. And then forsaking sin, and living a life that's pleasing to God. Finney put it this way: "Repentance is a change of *willing*, of *feeling* and of *living*, in respect to God."

This is hard—but let's face the truth: Repentance is not lip service. Repentance is seeing the blackness of our sin, and saying to God, "I realize how much pain I've caused you. Because of my sin, I was one of those who helped drive the nails into your flesh and bones." It's only when we see that our sin cost Him blood that we can turn away from ourselves and willingly live to please God. That is why John the Baptist said we needed to bring forth fruit in keeping with repentance (Matthew 3:8). That's why Paul reminded the people he preached to that they should prove their repentance by their deeds (Acts 26:20). Repentance has to come from the heart. Then it produces a changed life—tangible evidence to God, to us and to those around us that we have truly repented.

So how does true repentance occur? I believe it has to be a work of the Holy Spirit. Why? Because we're blinded by our sin, and we think we're a lot better than we really are. Only God sees into every crevice of our heart. He knows the filth that's piled up there. He wants us to see it as He sees it—and to decide we're going to get rid of it. I'm speaking of things like selfishness, anger, jealousy, self-pity, lust and possessiveness. Peace comes when we get honest with ourselves about the sin that's piled up in our heart—and ask God to remove it. Then we become clean before the Lord.

MaryAnn is a young woman who spent some time living in one of our homes. During her stay, she told us that her father had sexually abused her as a child. But since she'd become a Christian, she said it didn't bother her anymore. She said she'd forgiven her father for what he had done to her. She'd even written him to tell him so. Everything seemed nice and neat and sweet—until the Holy Spirit began to show MaryAnn the *real* condition of her heart.

As she was praying one day, she closed her eyes and saw her father's face. Immediately, she felt tremendous hatred for him. Before this time, MaryAnn tried to pretend she didn't hate her father because, after all, she was a Christian. Christians don't feel hate—right? Now she could feel this rage and for the first time she knew that in her heart she'd murdered her father many times for what he did to her. All this time she kept blindly saying, "Oh, I forgive him. I'm fine with God." But the Holy Spirit finally showed her how this hatred was holding her father in bondage. And how this sin had come between her and God.

That was when MaryAnn's pain over what was in her heart finally came out. She wept and wept. And then she repented of her sin. She immediately wrote her father another letter. This time she asked him to forgive *her* for her hatred and unwillingness to forgive him. She realized

---

Examine thoroughly the state of your hearts and see where you are, whether you walk daily with God or with the devil...You must determine to examine your sins.

—Charles Finney

---

that if she continued in bitterness, she would be eaten away by it. This did not in any way condone her father's sin or release him from its consequences if he continued to be unrepentant. But it did free the Holy Spirit to work in his life in a greater way. And it lifted a burden MaryAnn had carried for years.

Do you see what I'm driving at? It's so easy to whitewash our sins. So easy to bury them in some dark corner of our hearts and hope that nobody ever finds them. That's what MaryAnn did. She was only set free when the Holy Spirit shone his light into her heart so she could see the sin that was really there. Not until she saw it could she repent of it. Today she is still free and walking in victory because of that repentance.

But many Christians are in bondage because they haven't experienced the true freedom that MaryAnn found. Why? Because no one has explained to them what repentance does for you. No one has told them about dealing ruthlessly with sin so they can be free from it at last!

When I first came to the Lord I didn't understand repentance at all. So I spent a lot of time seeking counsel. I'd say to the counselor, "I don't feel saved. There are so many areas where I'm failing. I'm weak and frustrated."

And a counselor might say, "Oh, that's just the devil condemning you. You have to resist him, and believe Jesus loves you."

"Yeah," I'd say, "but I'm rotten in all those areas. And I don't have any peace. I'm making a mess of things. How can I really be saved?"

"*Of course* you're saved," he'd tell me. "We all make mistakes sometimes. Don't listen to those lies. God says you're free now. You have to receive that by faith."

Sometimes people use the word *faith* to mean *pretend*—you know, like saying, "I'm set free *by faith*," and then pretending you're free when you're not. That isn't faith. That's a sad joke.

So every counselling session would end with me resolving to pray harder and trying to exercise more faith.

And I *would!* I'd pray harder. I would read my Bible every day. But the next week I was right back at the same spot. One day, I couldn't stand it any longer. I said to Melody, "I don't care if I rot in here, I'm not coming out of the house until I have the peace of God."

I buried my face in the mattress and cried out to God with all my heart and soul: "Lord, I can't stand my hypocrisy any more. I can't stand any longer acting like it's revival time in my heart when I have no peace. What's my problem?"

Then the Holy Spirit shined His light into my heart. *Don't you see?* He said to me. *Your pride has told you that your sin is just a part of your personality. Your pride has allowed you to believe that these weak areas are something you'll have to learn to accept. But that's not the truth. You are a sinner, and you need to repent.*

And I said to the Lord, "Yes, but we're all sinners. I'm just a general sinner. Nobody's perfect!"

The Lord's rebuke stopped me in my tracks: *Don't make excuses. You are a sinner.* Then He began to show me that what I felt was His conviction. God was trying to lead me to repentance—and I'd been rebuking the devil instead!

What I didn't know—because no one had told me—was how to

embrace the whole message of salvation. I had not faced my sin and repented of it. That day I did, and my life began to change.

Do you understand the conviction of the Holy Spirit, or do you mistake it for the condemnation of the devil? We rebuke the devil. We do spiritual warfare. But nothing changes, because we haven't recognized that it may be the Holy Spirit working hard to get our attention. He wants to show us the condition of our heart. He wants to point out sins hidden away in dark corners—sins we don't want to admit. We can become free only when we own up to them, and repent.

David gives some insight on this,

> When I kept silent about my sin, my body wasted away through my groaning all day long. For day and night Thy hand was heavy upon me; my vitality was drained away as with the fever heat of summer. I acknowledged my sin to Thee, and my iniquity I did not hide; I said, "I will confess my transgressions to the Lord"; and Thou didst forgive the guilt of my sin (Psalm 32:3-5).

"Thy hand was heavy upon me." That sounds like conviction of sin. What did David do about it? He repented of his sin. He confessed it to the Lord and received forgiveness. So his guilt was taken away.

The Holy Spirit wants to convict us so we can repent and be restored. The devil wants to demoralize us and ultimately destroy us. The difference is simple: The Holy Spirit is always *specific*. He says, "Quit yelling at your kids," or "You need to pray more." On the other hand, the devil is *general* in his accusations. He says things like "You're a terrible parent and a lousy, prayerless Christian. Why don't you just give up!"

It's important to know who is talking to us so we can have the right response.

Here is what happens when we're faced with the conviction of the Holy Spirit and we don't respond in the right way: Let's say you begin to rebuke the devil instead of recognizing God at work. If that doesn't make you feel any better, you start making excuses: "Well I'm not so bad." Or "I try to live a good life." Or "I get it right ninety percent of the time." And then there is the great excuse of our time—you see it on bumper stickers everywhere: "Christians aren't perfect, just forgiven."

Sure, Christians are forgiven. But if that's where we have stopped, then we've short-changed God. God wants to perfect us so we can be light to the world. He wants to make us holy, not just forgiven.

When it came to repentance, King Saul was a great excuse-maker. Samuel, the prophet, delivered the word of the Lord to Saul—he was to fight against and utterly destroy the Amalekites. Everything, right down to their sheep, oxen and goats, was to be destroyed. Sure, Saul went to battle, but he decided to take the king of the Amalekites, Agag, as a captive—to show off as a prisoner of war. Saul was on a glory trip. And he allowed his men to take the best sheep and oxen, to prove how great and generous he was.

When Samuel heard what Saul had done, he cried out all night to the Lord. And the Lord said, "I regret that I have made Saul king, for he has turned back from following Me, and has not carried out My commands" (1 Samuel 15:11).

When Samuel confronted Saul about disobeying God, Saul started making excuses: "Come on, Samuel, it's not such a big deal. We just kept a few sheep and oxen. They're the best livestock we could find. In fact, we were going to use them as an offering to God!"

The Lord isn't impressed by our excuses because He sees the sin deep in our hearts. He wants obedience, not excuses. In Saul's case, Samuel said, "As a result of your disobedience and lack of repentance you're going to lose your throne." Later, the Lord raised up David to be king and Saul's life ended in defeat.

Where do we get this idea—that God will accept excuses for sin? The *only* thing He accepts for sin is repentance—because repentance separates us from the sin that's killing us spiritually! But we live in such an excuse-ridden world that making excuses for sin seems the easiest, most natural thing to do. God expects us to take responsibility for *our* sin, and leave other people to Him. Sure, many of us have hurts and scars from the past. But God can heal those hurts and give us a new start. He longs to renew us from within. But He can't do it unless we stop making excuses and start taking responsibility for our actions.

You see, there won't be a third option on Judgment Day. It's not going to be yes, no, or best excuse. It's going to be yes I did that, or no I didn't. Yes I repented of my sin, or no I didn't. That's God's standard. Don't find out the hard way that God doesn't tolerate excuses.

Christians wonder why they continue to live in pain or confusion or have no sense of direction. Some of them blame it on God. But you see,

He wants to make us clean—and then He can pour His living water through us. Rivers of it, like He promised!

Maybe no one told us *accepting the Lord means rejecting sin.* Think about it. If you want a glass of water to drink, what's the first thing you do? You make sure the glass is clean. If you pour clean water into a dirty glass, the water loses its purity. It's no longer fit to drink. It's the same with the Holy Spirit. The Holy Spirit can't be poured into this world through an unclean vessel.

We are taught to clean up our *behavior*—emphasis is placed on outward appearance, the part of us that others see. So a lot of us look all bright and shiny on the outside—we seem to have everything together—but on the inside we're full of crud. But the Holy Spirit sees it because He looks on the heart—that's where He's going to dwell.

It's as if He comes and inspects the premises. He wants to see if we've cleaned up so He can move in. And when He finds we haven't, He gets on our case. He brings conviction. He tries to get our attention. But if we continually ignore Him, or try to push Him away with excuses, we'll keep heading into darkness—all the while blaming God for not rescuing us! But if we acknowledge Him, He'll work within us to clean up our heart. If we repent of our sin and make some deliberate decisions to live differently, He will forgive us our sins and He'll move in to take up residence in our new heart. And once He's residing there, He gives us the power we need to live a godly life.

Now here's the big challenge—are you ready? Sometimes we have to clean up things we don't want to. There's a battle of wills going on—God's will, or ours. There may be some sins there that are painful to face. Some that require us to make restitution for something we stole, or ask forgiveness from someone we've wronged. Life may suddenly seem dark and stormy, but we find this promise in Psalms:

> For His anger is but for a moment, His favor is for a lifetime; weeping may last for the night, but a shout of joy comes in the morning (Psalm 30:5).

Joy comes in the morning—and peace and the other fruits of the Spirit. All of it comes as a result of a repentant heart and a righteous lifestyle. Fruit doesn't come from nowhere. You don't plant an apple seed one day and pick apples the next. You've got to cultivate, water, fertilize and prune. And if the process is done right, you get some fruit. The fruit of the Spirit comes through the process of repentance. We cultivate our hearts—plow them up, make them soft by repentance. And the Holy Spirit waters, tends and brings fruit—a harvest of righteousness.

The fruit of the Spirit will be our reward.

Jesus said,

"*…He who*
hates his life
  in this world
     shall keep it
  to life eternal."

John 12:25

Consider
Yourself Dead

We have been buried with [Christ Jesus] through baptism into death, in order that as Christ was raised from the dead through the glory of the Father, so we too might walk in newness of life (Romans 6:4).

———————————◆———————————

When Melody and I first became Christians, we felt we'd been adopted into a huge new family. We met wonderful new grandparents, parents and older brothers and sisters in the Lord. We never knew such a great family existed before we met the Lord. We had no idea about Christian love, fellowship and support, and suddenly we were surrounded by people who loved Jesus and loved us. We wanted to love them all right back!

Whenever we met anyone who was even remotely interested in knowing about Jesus, we introduced them to our new family. We wanted them to see the reality of Christ at work in the lives of all these people. Since we were new Christians, we figured that these older Christians could answer all the questions and radiate Christ at the same time—that is, until we went over to Leo's house.

We were looking for some Christian friends that day, hoping they could talk to a woman we'd met and help answer some of her questions about the Lord. We were told they were at Leo's. What a sad surprise for us. At Leo's, the party was in full swing. People were lying all over the floor, tripping out on drugs or guzzling beer. We recognized some people from our Bible study. Our hearts hit the floor! Here were people we respected, obviously in no condition to witness to anyone. Melody and I walked out of the party stunned. The woman with us was disillusioned and our idealistic little world was shattered.

Man, were we confused. It was as if we didn't really know these people after all. Like they had two lives—one life they wore, like a suit of clothes, at Bible studies, and another life they wore for their secular friends. You know, a "church suit" and a "pagan suit."

I have seen many Christians since then who are on fire for the Lord one minute, but cool off fast when unsaved friends are around. They're not on fire, they're just playing with fire. A lot of these people come up to me after concerts and ask for counsel and prayer and help. Dozens of them. Hundreds. They don't like it when I point out that no one can help them unless they're willing to stop living double lives.

Here are a few examples. I have pleaded with Christian music artists who have live-in girlfriends; with "Spirit-filled" Christians who won't give up their booze; with friends who get a high from Jesus on Sunday and a high from drugs on Monday. These are people who know the Word of God and who represent that Word to others—and at the same time they are trading on the grace of God. They are hoping He will be waiting for them when they decide to get their act together.

Unless they see the deeper truth, though, they're headed for a big crash. Paul knew what to do to the "old man" inside each of us—the old life that tries to kill God's Spirit in us:

> Reckon ye also yourselves to be dead indeed unto sin
> (Romans 6:11, KJV).

What does it mean to *reckon* ourselves dead to sin?

The word *reckon* means to "calculate, compute, regard, consider with confidence, rely, count or base your plans upon." Paul is saying, "Don't *plan* on sinning any more. Think of yourselves as being dead to sin." That means, don't snort cocaine. Stop lying. Quit going out with the men or women who'll tempt you into bed. Don't steal anymore. You're dead to all that sin. It's over. It's no longer a choice for you, so don't even toy with it.

Does this mean it's impossible for people who have Christ living in them to sin? No, we don't become robots when we accept Christ. Each of us is very capable of sinning. But when we reckon ourselves dead to sin, we recognize that sin is no longer our master. We are no longer compelled to sin, no longer held hostage by it. There *is* a way out, because Jesus has become our new master and Lord.

Reckoning ourselves dead to sin is the next step once the Holy Spirit convicts us of sin. We look at our behavior and say, "That is spiritual death." We don't say, "Well...I guess it's not so good. Maybe I should stop. Sometime. When it's not fun anymore, or it hurts someone." *No.* We have to choose a new path. We base our plans upon the belief that we are dead to sin. We stop choosing sin, and choose instead to make choices that lead to life.

The question for a lot of people is, how do I make the right choice, when this old habit seems to have a hold on me?

Every day we're presented with choices. For example, God tells us to serve. So we start doing what God has told us to do—maybe at home, at work or in a ministry. About this time our flesh sneaks up and says, "I'm so disappointed. Nobody knows how hard I'm working. Nobody appreciates what I'm doing. Nobody cares at all about me. They just like me for what I can do. I'm being used."

Sometimes Satan gets in on the act, too. He comes to us as a whiney little voice in our mind and starts planting sorry thoughts there. Every one of his negative thoughts is like an arrow that shoots us down from what God has clearly told us to do.

And here's the place where we can decide to give life to our old, self-centered flesh or put it to death so we can walk in our new God-centered spiritual life. We can say, "I agree with what my flesh is telling me. These people probably are using me." So we bring that thought to the front of our mind, entertain it, act on it. When we do this we enter into sin. Or we can say, "I serve God—not other men. He is building something into my life through serving—even when no one notices. 'It is more blessed to give than to receive'" (Acts 20:35).

So we do have a choice in reckoning ourselves dead to sin. That's what "dying with Jesus" means. *Spiritually,* death with Christ is imputed to us once for all at salvation. But *practically,* we have to live it out daily in our lives. Paul said he had to die daily (1 Corinthians 15:31). Every day he came to a crossroads in his life where he had to choose life in Christ over sin and death.

So on one side, we have our flesh, the devil, the world, our old friends, the media all urging us to make wrong choices. On the other side, we have God urging us to make righteous choices. It's a giant tug-of-war. This tension can leave us feeling worse than before we became Christians.

We need to take an honest look at this, because this tension is real. It's as if there are two teams—the flesh and the Holy Spirit—living within one body. Paul talked a lot about this struggle. In his letter to the Galatians he listed the goals of the two teams that war within us:

> For the flesh sets its desire against the Spirit, and the Spirit against the flesh; for these are in opposition to one another, so that you may not do the things that you please...Now the deeds of the flesh are evident, which are: immorality, impurity, sensuality, idolatry, sorcery, enmities, strife, jealousy, outbursts of anger, disputes, dissensions, factions, envying, drunkenness, carousing, and things like these...But the fruit of the Spirit is love, joy, peace, patience, kindness, goodness, faithfulness, gentleness, self-control; against such things there is no law (Galatians 5:17-23).

I've surely experienced this in my life. There is no common ground between the flesh and the Spirit—in my life or yours. This leaves us with a dilemma. We know what we *need* to do, yet we can't seem to get our

---◆---

Abide in Jesus, the sinless one—which means, give up all of self and its life, and dwell in God's will and rest in His strength. This is what brings the power that does not commit sin.

—Andrew Murray

---◆---

bodies to do it. Every day I do a hundred things that I don't want to do: I react negatively to people. I give in to bad attitudes. I use a sarcastic tone of voice. The things I don't want to do, I do. And the things I want to do, I seem unable to accomplish. Paul said it like this:

I find then the principle that evil is present in me, the one who wishes to do good. For I joyfully concur with the law of God in the inner man, but I see a different law in the members of my body, waging war against the law of my mind, and making me a prisoner of the law of sin which is in my members (Romans 7:21-23).

Paul says this fight that's taking place inside of him drives him crazy:

Wretched man that I am! Who will set me free from the body of this death? (Romans 7:24).

You can feel Paul getting weary in the battle, can't you? Losing strength. Wanting to lie down and give up. Where do we get the strength to win? Paul answers his own question:

Thanks be to God through Jesus Christ our Lord! (Romans 7:25)

The only way we will ever subdue our flesh and allow Jesus to be victorious in our life is to let God work in us. First, we have to make the right decision—that's our part. When God created us, He gave us a will. God gave something to man that He gave to no other creature. Take dogs, for example. Dogs do what their instinct tells them to do. When it's mating time, a dog goes out and finds a partner. They mate and have puppies. The female dog doesn't think, *I wonder what kind of a dad he'll make.* Or, *Is this the color coat I want my puppies to have?* Dogs don't think about those things. They were made to simply do what their instinct has programed them to do. But it's not like that for us. We have choices to make. We're not ruled by our instinct.

God has given you the choice of how you live your life. Your will—and mine—is the only thing in the universe God does not own. In this area, and this area only, He has humbled himself and allowed another creature to make decisions that affect Him. There are many times in the Bible where it is recorded that God felt anger, disappointment, regret or sorrow—all because He gave us the choice of how we live our lives. But He won't take control of our wills by force. If we want Him to have control of our lives, we must give that control to Him. If we choose to go it alone we're doomed to failure. We need God's help.

In our first few years in California, the Lord sent two girls who'd been involved in drugs and prostitution to live with us. Although they weren't tempted to run off and become prostitutes again, the freewheeling life of drug-taking, going to wild parties and breaking all the rules was often hard for them to resist. On more than one occasion we had to lay down the law. But it paid off. They had some setbacks, but over the years they consistently yielded their wills to the Lord and made right choices. Bit by bit their lives were transformed by God. If you met them today, you'd never guess the kind of background they'd had.

When we lay our life and our will on God's altar, nothing is impossible. When we use our will to make godly choices, we free God to be our partner. When we turn our whole heart towards Him and step out in faith, He moves heaven and earth to see that we have victory over our flesh.

It's like the story of the prodigal son that Jesus told in Luke 15. There was only one thing the father would not do for his son. He would not send his servant out to find his son and drag him home. Why? Because he knew he had let his son make his own choice. The son had to recognize where his new lifestyle was leading him—down to a pigsty, and death. He had to humble himself and turn his face towards home. But once the son made that choice, got up and got within sight of home—an uproar began! His father rushed out to welcome him. He gave his son a robe and a ring and then threw a big homecoming party.

God is the same with us. We have a war going on within us. A war between our flesh and the Spirit of God. It's our choice which side we will throw the weight of our will into. If we want to pull for the side of sin and death, we can do that. But we also have the Spirit of Christ within, bringing life and hope and righteousness in our bodies. He is waiting—eagerly, like the prodigal son's father—to give us the power and authority we need to stand against temptation.

God's only condition is that we make the choice to turn from temptation. As Paul says, we must reckon ourselves dead to our own desires.

Paul told the Philippians:

> ...I count all things to be loss in view of the surpassing value of knowing Christ Jesus my Lord, for whom I have suffered the loss of all things, and count them but rubbish in order

that I may gain Christ, and may be found in Him, not having a righteousness of my own derived from the Law, but that which is through faith in Christ, the righteousness which comes from God on the basis of faith, that I may know Him, and the power of His resurrection (Philippians 3:8-10).

We need to live in the power of the resurrection—a power that's at our disposal if we set our hearts to follow Christ. One of Paul's prayers for the Ephesians was:

I pray that the eyes of your heart may be enlightened, so that you may know what is the hope of His calling, what are the riches of the glory of His inheritance in the saints, and what is the *surpassing greatness of His power* toward us who believe (Ephesians 1:18-19, emphasis added).

When Paul talks about the resurrection power of Jesus, he is talking about the ultimate power source! And that power source is available to us. When we make a conscious choice to obey the Spirit of God within us and resist our flesh, the power switch is turned on. The power of God is released in us. He gives us the power to live righteously.

There is another word for this power that comes when we reckon ourselves dead to sin. The word is *grace*. Grace is the infinite, patient strength of God working in our human spirits. Grace is what sets us apart as believers. People who aren't Christians can read the Bible to find out what God requires. But they can never do what God wants in their own strength. They don't have the grace of God within them.

Therefore having been justified by faith, we have peace with God through our Lord Jesus Christ, through whom also we have obtained our introduction by faith into this grace in which we stand; and we exult in hope of the glory of God (Romans 5:1-2).

If we have Christ *in* us, we stand in grace. It's as though we were standing in the powerful currents of the ocean. Grace surrounds us. It moves us. Every way we look, there is grace. It is impossible to live out the gospel in our own strength. It is all-important that we rely on the power and grace of God so we can live our lives day after day without burning out.

You see, grace is like the oil in an engine. When Henry Ford put his first engine together, he probably looked at all the pieces of metal and said to himself, "How am I going to keep this thing from grinding itself into dust in two hours?" And someone said, "Oil."

In a similar way, we go to God and say, "How am I going to live this life? How am I going to overcome the opposite impulses going on inside of me? How do I keep these forces from grinding me down?" And God says, "The oil of the Spirit. The Spirit of Grace will keep you from burning up and grinding to a halt."

God is so patient—so full of grace. When Christ lives within us, He gives us the power to choose righteousness. God reaches down in grace and takes our hand. Together, there is no sin, no temptation we cannot conquer.

Then we begin to see the truth of Paul's promise, "It is no longer I who live, but Christ lives in me" (Galatians 2:20). And he also said:

> Now if we have died with Christ, we believe that we shall also live with Him, knowing that Christ, having been raised from the dead, is never to die again; death no longer is master over Him. For the death that He died, He died to sin, once for all; but the life that He lives, He lives to God (Romans 6:8–10).

Constantly—daily—go before God and ask, "Please awaken the new me. And bury the old me in a grave. I don't want to have any more to do with the old me."

If you have never done this before, do it now. Consider yourself dead to sin, and alive to Christ.

You'll see how the eternal power of God—made available to us by the finished work of the cross—will help you to walk in resurrection life.

Jesus said,

"*Keep watching and praying,*

that you

may not come

into temptation;

the spirit is willing,

but the flesh is weak."

Mark 14:38

Stand 4
Against The Enemy

Resist the devil and he will flee from you (James 4:7).

Since then we have a great high priest who…has been tempted in all things as we are, yet without sin (Hebrews 4:14-15).

———————◆———————

Does the Bible really mean what it says—that Jesus "has been tempted in all things as we are"?

After His baptism, Jesus was led by the Spirit out into the wilderness, where He fasted and prayed for forty days. And at the end, when He was very weak, the devil came to tempt Him (Luke 4:1-13). Look at this closely, because the devil used three different strategies to try to seduce Jesus to sin.

The first strategy played on Jesus' need for physical sustenance. "If You are the Son of God, tell this stone to become bread" (4:3). Satan used the word *if* in an attempt to goad Jesus into proving He was indeed the Son of God—a fact that Satan already knew well!

The second temptation offered a quick way for Jesus to "own" the earth. The devil showed Him all the kingdoms of the world in a moment of time. Then he said to Jesus, "I will give You all this domain and its glory; for it has been handed over to me, and I give it to whomever I wish. Therefore if You worship before me, it shall all be Yours" (4:6-7). This time Satan offered Jesus the cheap, easy way out—a way to get what He wanted without all the fuss and bother, all the agony and blood of the crucifixion.

The third temptation was an attempt to get Jesus to tempt God himself. The devil took Jesus to the pinnacle of the temple in Jerusalem, and said to Him, "If You are the Son of God, throw Yourself down from here; for it is written, 'He will give His angels charge concerning You to guard You'" (4:9-10).

But each time, Jesus resisted the devil until he gave up and withdrew. Even in His weakened physical state, Jesus would not give in to any of the temptations. His heart was found to be pure. You think that Satan would have quit. No way.

Luke says:

> And when the devil had finished every temptation, he departed from [Jesus] until an opportune time (Luke 4:13).

That's a statement we've got to look at—*an opportune time.* What does it mean? Obviously, the devil was not going to let the whole matter drop. He was going to keep an eye on things, waiting to see if there was a moment when Jesus would let down His guard. Maybe there would be one moment when His flesh might be exposed—and if ever that occurred, Satan was ready to pounce....

Scripture shows us that even for Jesus, temptation wasn't a onetime battle. You know, resist once and it's over. Resisting the devil is not a onetime thing for any of us. Satan is always on the lookout for an opportune time to get at us. He might wait until, like Jesus, we are at a low point physically. Or he might wait until we've reached some spiritual milestone—so he can lure us into pride and independence.

What would be the most opportune time for Satan to tempt you away from serving God? How would he do it? You and I need to answer these questions. Because when we decide to be a disciple of Jesus, we can expect the same treatment from His old adversary the devil. We'll never beat the devil by ignoring him. That's why we need to be aware of his tactics and ready to resist him every day. How can we be sure we don't leave any area exposed for the devil to prey on? Let's look at some Scriptures that tell us how to keep from giving him an opportune time.

The biggest mistake we can make is to think we have power to resist the devil when we're out of relationship with Jesus. If we're not *in* Christ, if we're not walking by the Spirit, we're sitting ducks.

When Paul was in Ephesus, miracles were happening. People were healed, demons were cast out. There were some young guys, seven brothers, who watched all of this and were amazed. They decided that if Paul could do it, so could they. They memorized what Paul said and looked for someone to try it out on. Along came a demon-possessed man, and they began casting the evil spirit out of him in Jesus' name. Big mistake! Luke tells us:

> But also some of the Jewish exorcists, who went from place to place, attempted to name over those who had the evil spirits the name of the Lord Jesus, saying, "I adjure you by Jesus whom Paul preaches." And seven sons of one Sceva, a Jewish chief priest, were doing this. And the evil spirit answered and said to them, "I recognize Jesus, and I know about Paul, but who are you?" And the man, in whom was the evil spirit, leaped on them and...overpowered them, so that they fled out of that house naked and wounded (Acts 19:13-16).

What a rude awakening for these seven guys! Think about it—the odds were seven-to-one in favor of the brothers. Even in the flesh they should have been able to take on one man. But the demon tore their clothes off and beat them all to bloody pulps.

They must have asked themselves, "How did this happen? Didn't we do everything that Paul did?" Yes, they did. But they were not everything that Paul *was.* You see, Jesus promised power to resist the devil in His name—but only to those who are His disciples (Mark 16:17).

Paul was a disciple of Jesus; the seven sons of Sceva were impostors. They had the right actions, but the wrong heart. And the demon knew it. He could tell in a second that they had no real authority. They were just using the name of Jesus for their own ends, without any understanding or concern for His kingdom.

What's the most important way to resist the devil? Set your heart on knowing Christ. The closer we are to Jesus, the less vulnerable we are to Satan. Even in the Old Testament we see this principle at work: "The name of the Lord is a strong tower; the righteous runs into it and is safe" (Proverbs 18:10). In times of attack, there is nothing better to do than to run into the strong tower of our relationship with the Lord—to trust in His Spirit. If we don't have that relationship, then we'll be just like the sons of Sceva, wondering why the enemy leaves us beaten and battered every time.

Second, we resist the devil by knowing his tactics. Peter says,

> Be of sober spirit, be on the alert. Your adversary, the devil, prowls about like a roaring lion, seeking someone to devour (1 Peter 5:8).

Many Christians think that if we ignore the devil he'll go away. This is wishful thinking. You can't find this idea anywhere in Scripture. Just the opposite is true. Throughout the Bible, there are references and warnings about Satan's works and strategies.

Let's take the temptation of Jesus in the wilderness. We know that He was alone when Satan came, so we have to assume He told His disciples about the experience later. Why? Because He wanted to alert them—and us—to the patterns of deceit Satan uses.

So when Peter tells us to be sober and on the alert, what should we watch for? Peter calls him a lion. Don't ever forget the devil is a scavenger. He feeds on wounded and vulnerable people. People who have strayed from the safe sheepfold because some area of their lives is not fully submitted to Christ. Maybe it starts with a little bitterness stored up in the heart. Maybe there's a little wounded pride. Or arrogance—we think we can ignore wise counsel. You separate yourself in spirit—and Satan attacks.

Here's where the Holy Spirit comes in to shed light, and to protect us. We need to ask Him to give us an honest look at ourselves. Moving away from fellowship and protection tends to lead us back toward areas of sin and weakness where the devil attacks.

For example, maybe you feel bored with your spiritual life, or angry at a brother. You begin to think all this Christianity stuff is a waste of time. But you think it secretly—no one knows. If you have problems with lust or sexual immorality, you might begin to hang around adult book stores. Oh sure, you just go to look, not buy—right? If you've been into alcohol, you pick up some wine—an expensive bottle! After all, you're no wino!

What happens is that you've moved in your spirit—from commitment to messing with sin again. To see how close you can come to the fire without being burned.

In both of his letters to Timothy, Paul offers the same advice:

> But flee from these [sinful] things, you man of God; and

pursue righteousness, godliness, faith, love, perseverance and gentleness (1 Timothy 6:11).

...flee from youthful lusts, and pursue righteousness, faith, love and peace, with those who call on the Lord from a pure heart (2 Timothy 2:22).

Flee. That means run. Flee from everything that gives Satan a claw-hold on your life. Where do we run? We should run after righteousness, godliness, gentleness, faith and love. And where do we find those things? In the Lord.

It comes back to pursuing God. Seeking Him daily, giving ourselves to Him.

By doing this, as Paul told the Ephesians, we won't give the devil "an opportunity" (Ephesians 4:27).

Before I leave this point, I'll tell you why I put it first: Because a lot of Christians have never put much distance between themselves and the things that pulled them into sin. They don't see sin as that serious.

I compare sin to venereal disease—I know it's not the most delicate of examples, but it's accurate. A person gets VD from having so-called "fun." The first signs of it are hard to detect and almost painless. But then it takes root in their body and, if left untreated, eventually blinds them, drives them crazy and finally kills them. Sin is like that. It seems fun, but

---◆---

The inward area is the first place of loss of true Christian life, of true spirituality, and the outward sinful act is the result.

—Francis Schaeffer

---◆---

it's sinister fun—like swallowing a sugar-coated, time-release cyanide capsule. A little bit of compromise here, a little bit there. It's hard to see how it's all piling up in our lives. But it's there, and it's deadly. Playing games with sin can destroy our lives—spiritually and physically.

But once we put some distance between us and sin, we can see things more clearly, think more clearly. That's where the "full armor of God" comes in.

The Ephesians were surrounded by pagan idol-worship and sick lifestyles. It's no wonder Paul told them,

> Put on the full armor of God, that you may be able to stand firm against the schemes of the devil (Ephesians 6:11).

In Paul's day, soldiers had to wear a lot of armor to do battle—helmet, breastplate, shoes, shield. If you left off even one piece, you were vulnerable. If you were smart, you didn't go to battle without a breastplate. If you did, you were begging for someone to shoot you in the heart with an arrow. A smart soldier—one who lived to tell about the battle—made sure to have *all* his armor on.

Let's go over Paul's list of spiritual armor.

First, we're to have our loins girded with truth (Ephesians 6:14). God's Word is His truth. That means we have to read it, learn it, memorize it, have it ready when Satan attacks. That's what Jesus did when He was tempted—He turned back the devil's advances with the Word of truth. He fought off temptation with Scripture. Remember when the devil tempted Him to turn stones into bread? He responded by quoting Deuteronomy 8:3: "Man does not live by bread alone, but man lives by everything that proceeds out of the mouth of the Lord." Can you see it? Satan was knocked back a few steps. The truth drove him off, so he knew he couldn't penetrate Jesus' spiritual armor that way.

Do you have the Word of God stored in your heart, ready to protect yourself whenever Satan attacks?

Paul also tells us about the breastplate of righteousness (6:14). Now this is not *our* righteousness. Our righteousness is as filthy rags. The only thing that will protect our hearts is *God's* righteousness. The devil can come to us and say, "Look at you. You've blown it again. You're never going to get it right, are you?" And we can say, "That's not true. I am growing in Christ slowly, every day. And there is no condemnation because I'm in Christ Jesus."

We're also to have our feet shod with the preparation of the gospel of peace (4:15). There's no better way to resist the devil than to use his own attack as an opportunity to advance the gospel. How wonderful to take a situation that Satan sets to trap us and use it to declare the gospel and win others to the Lord.

The story of Robert, a new believer, illustrates this point. In Robert's high school physical education class the coach announced that the following week they'd be going out on the track to jump high hurdles. Robert was not only unathletic, he was also overweight—and he knew what was going to happen. He was probably going to trip and land face-first on the asphalt and give the whole class one more chance to laugh at him. When the day came, a group of the guys cut class, forging fake notes from their parents. Robert wanted to cut too and save himself the pain and embarrassment. But he knew it wasn't right, and he knew that if the other guys in his class saw him cutting out it would be a bad witness. So he stuck it out—and didn't do too badly, just one or two falls. No broken bones. And nobody laughed at him.

A couple of weeks later, a guy from the class said to Robert, "I thought for sure you were going to cut class like all the other guys. But you stuck it out, even though you knew you were going to bite the dust. Why?"

Robert saw it as a chance to talk about his relationship with Jesus Christ—and the other guy got saved that day! You see, Robert could have given into the temptation to lie. But he stood his ground, did what was right and then he could speak with integrity about Christ. The other guy knew that Robert really believed what he said, and God used that as a witness to get into his heart that day.

Then there's the shield of faith (4:16). God's shield is not something we hide behind. It's something we use aggressively. When the flaming darts of the enemy come screaming in, we can swing our shield and deflect them. Our shield is *faith*—the unshakable certainty we have that God is who He says He is, and that He's done for us all He said He'd do. Satan's lies can't get to us when we trust God. That kind of faith extinguishes all Satan's flaming arrows.

Then we need the helmet of salvation and the sword of the Spirit (4:17). The helmet protects the head, which controls the whole body. Satan knows that whoever controls the mind controls the body. To stand against his attack we have to get the knowledge of our salvation into our heads. Day by day, we surrender to God and He cleanses our minds. He takes away the junk, the old thought-patterns. As these are taken away, the devil loses his foothold there.

And the sword of the Spirit, Paul tells us, is the Word of God. When we get our heads straight about God, and really believe His Word, then it becomes our sword for attacking. A sword is what you wield in battle to attack and overcome the enemy. If you want to make it as a Christian disciple, you've got to be ready, with your sword sharpened for the attack.

Remember, the devil looks for people who are sick and weak in spirit. He's reluctant to attack anyone who's armed and ready—anyone who can fight back. Why should he put his energy into a fight he knows he's already lost?

One final point about our spiritual weapons. Paul also says,

> With all prayer and petition pray at all times in the Spirit, and with this in view, be on the alert with all perseverance and petition for all the saints (Ephesians 6:18).

Prayer is our ultimate weapon. But we can be so foolish when we're attacked by the devil. Prayer is the first thing we let drop! We run around to all our friends and whine, "Oh, I'm under attack. Lay hands on me! Pray for me!" When we're attacked we should stand our ground and pray harder. Sure, it's okay to ask our brothers and sisters for their prayer support. But prayer is the lifeline that keeps us connected to God. If our lifeline is cut, the devil's victory is inevitable. But if we stay plugged into God, who is our life, then we'll always win over our adversary the devil. Finally—and this is an important point—we have to learn how to live "in the light." John says,

> If we walk in the light as [God] Himself is in the light, we have fellowship with one another, and the blood of Jesus His Son cleanses us from all sin (1 John 1:7).

That sounds pretty spiritual, but what does it mean? What is walking in the light?

For one thing, practically, it is living honestly with God, letting Him show us the truth about ourselves and our hidden motives. It also means seeking help with weak areas—being willing to be accountable to other Christians. You know, we all fake it some of the time—and some Christians seem to fake it a lot of the time. Everything seems so nice and spiritual on the outside, but on the inside things aren't pretty. We're a mess. There's sin and wickedness inside and we try to hide it. But eventually we can't fake it any more. We can't hold things together; the pressure gets too great and the true state of our heart comes out. Maybe we've been pretending to be spiritual and patient with someone. But one day all our criticalness and anger bursts out.

But it doesn't have to be that way. We don't have to fake it. We can choose to walk in the light. That means daily letting others see the weak state of our heart. That's humility—allowing others to see our weakness. We do it so that they can encourage us, support us and hold us accountable in that area. When we live this way, John tells us we can enjoy true fellowship with one another.

Not only that, we can bring things into the light and ask God to forgive us of our sin. Sin is always at the root, isn't it? And John says God is faithful to forgive us *and* cleanse us (1 John 1:9).

Do you see the whole thing now? With our sin forgiven, and with others supporting us and holding us accountable, there's not much left for the devil to get hold of, is there? There's nothing we're hiding in dark corners that we don't want others to see. No secret sin buried away. No weak flesh exposed for the prowling lion to jump on.

A lot of people like to spout all the Scriptures about our "birthright"—our total victory over Satan. But that total victory hasn't come yet. There's a spiritual war to be fought. Any disciple of Jesus who isn't in some kind of spiritual warfare probably isn't willing to be on the front lines! Maybe you're looking for comfort and blessing and don't want to get out there where lost people are being cut down by Satan.

You see, there's another way we can resist the devil. We go to war for the sake of other people, who will die and go to hell if we don't win them for Christ.

We like to quote that verse from James we looked at earlier—"Resist the devil and he will flee...." But we overlook the first part of it: "Submit therefore to God." That comes first.

Total submission to God. That's what is going to win the war against Satan. That's the key.

I meet Christians all the time who are more like the seven sons of Sceva than true disciples. They're about to turn their backs on God, some of them, because they got beaten up by the devil and they're offended at God. But most of them aren't honest with themselves. They refuse to run very far away from their sin. They don't take the time to know God's Word and arm themselves. And forget about regular prayer! They continue to live in pride, pretending they're doing fine spiritually, when really they're hiding secret sins. And on top of that, they're still living self-centered lives at the core of it all. They won't submit to God, who wants us to get free so we can help bring others out of darkness. All this resistance to God! And then they wonder why they're living defeated lives.

It doesn't make much sense, does it?

Jesus said,

" …God knows

your hearts."

Luke 16:15

Build
5
A Fire Of Holiness

And [Jesus] found in the temple those who were selling oxen and sheep and doves, and the moneychangers seated. And He made a scourge of cords, and drove them all out of the temple .... His disciples remembered that it was written, "Zeal for Thy house will consume me" (John 2:14–15,17).

———————◆———————

Imagine how the disciples felt watching their Master upsetting the lovely decorum of the temple. The noise, the dust, the shouting, the money spilling, the tables upturned—how dare He do such a thing! The disciples were probably shocked at first, then elated. That's how I would have felt. "Good job, Jesus! Show everyone who's boss!" When it was over, the disciples thought back to the Scripture that says, "Zeal for Thy house has consumed me" (Psalm 69:9). They thought, *Now we see what that means. Jesus loves his Father's house so deeply that he won't tolerate sin in it.*

No doubt Jesus' action that day excited everyone. The common people were thrilled to have a hero who could kick around all the religious windbags and money-grubbing scum. If it meant popularity—or flexing their muscles—the disciples were all for it. The only problem was, they didn't understand one fundamental fact about human nature: our *zeal* lacks direction.

Zeal is simply earnestness or fervor in advancing a cause. But that cause can be good or bad, focused or misguided. And as we read through the Gospels, we see that the disciples' zeal was often misguided.

The Pharisees were zealous, too—and also misguided. No one could say these guys didn't have zeal. *Everything* they did involved religious duties and doctrines. But their zeal was founded on legalism, not on knowing God. They promoted a cause that was cold and lifeless—a cause that made their hearts proud and arrogant.

We love to poke fun at the Pharisees. We like to read the rebukes that Jesus used to level them. But we're just as capable of misdirecting our zeal to useless religious activities. Things that are all for outward show—stuff that generates heat but not light.

That's how I was when I first became a Christian—I had lots of zeal. I never gave too much thought about where my energy was directed, and I did a few things that were pointless, ungodly and unproductive. They didn't advance my relationship with the Lord, or the Kingdom of God here on earth. We can all misdirect our zeal at times.

But some of us, like the Pharisees, get trapped by own own zealousness. We replace our relationship with the Lord with our "righteous" activity, and end up trying to earn our salvation by proving how zealous we are.

There are four ways Christians commonly misuse their zeal. They are: fighting causes that aren't God's causes, judging others, arguing over the Bible and seeking blessings more than the Giver of those blessings. I want to focus on these areas because they cause destructiveness and havoc in the body of Christ. Let's take a look at each of these four areas and see what true zeal for God is *not*.

First, we can be zealous for God yet totally miss His big picture. If we're not careful we can be zealous for causes that aren't God's at all.

Peter seemed to be the most zealous of the twelve disciples. Wherever there was trouble he was ready to jump in and save the day—at least in the flesh.

In the Garden of Gethsemane, Peter provided us with a perfect example of misplaced zeal. As the soldiers came to take Jesus away, Peter pulled out his sword and cut off the ear of the high priest's servant.

Jesus said to Peter, "Put your sword back into its place; for all those who take up the sword shall perish by the sword. Or do you think that I cannot appeal to My Father, and He will at once put at My disposal more than twelve legions of angels?" (Matthew 26:52-53).

What did Peter think he was doing? The same thing many of us think we're doing—protecting the Lord's reputation with ungodly methods, and hurting innocent people in the process. Peter, like the other disciples, totally missed God's big picture—His plan to send Jesus to the cross.

Peter had another plan. He still hoped Jesus would be the conquering hero. Sure, Peter had a lot of zeal for that. But he lacked the same zeal when it came to being a spiritual companion to Jesus. Peter, who was so courageous about swinging his sword in public, was the same guy who abandoned Jesus at the moment He took on His most difficult spiritual mission—humbling himself and going to the cross.

How is it that we're so zealous to put on outward, heroic shows of loyalty for our faith—and so reluctant to set aside our own agenda and do what Jesus wants us to do? Our zeal is misdirected. We need to transfer our zeal from outward things to inward spiritual things. We need to be less willing to cut off ears in Jesus' name, and more willing to humble ourselves, go into our prayer closet alone with Him and get *His* agenda for our lives.

Paul reminds us:

> The mind set on the flesh is hostile toward God; for it does not subject itself to the law of God, for it is not even able to do so; and those who are in the flesh cannot please God (Romans 8:7-8).

Much harm has been done to God's name by so-called spiritual battles waged in the flesh. Look at all the religious wars that have been fought, the crusades that have been carried out. All the blood and destruction. How could zeal be so misdirected? How could people think they were committing such atrocities in the name of God? But before standing in judgment of anyone else, we'd better realize we're all capable of pushing our own agenda ahead of God's agenda.

Second, we Christians have to admit that we have a problem—a bad habit of judging each other. In Luke 9, it says,

> [Jesus] sent messengers on ahead of Him. And they went, and entered a village of the Samaritans, to make arrangements for Him. And they did not receive Him, because He was journeying with His face toward Jerusalem. And when His disciples James and John saw this, they said, "Lord, do You want us to command fire to come down

from heaven and consume them?" But He turned and rebuked them (vv. 52-55).

I doubt that James and John were expecting a rebuke. Here was a whole village of people who had rejected Jesus—they deserved to be fried. They'd blown their chance to welcome Jesus. As far as these zealous disciples were concerned, it was time for this village to see the power of God.

How many times have you acted like James and John? How often do you become a judge, and bring down the gavel on someone who's obviously in the wrong? Some people have a lifelong preoccupation with sitting in judgment over every ministry, every elder, every pastor and every Bible study leader. They call down fire—bringing down the gavel of judgment hard and heavy. They say they're trying to bring correction, but they crush, kill and destroy.

I was once like that.

When I was a new Christian I opened up my Bible, then set myself up as judge. I'd go into ministries and get loud about their need for correction. Worse than that, within six months of my conversion I was on-stage performing. Thousands of people came to hear me, and I really got into letting them know what I thought—judging things publicly.

One day God grabbed me by the collar and showed me something: judgment comes out of spiritual immaturity. A mature Christian will pray, discern, love and counsel. If need be they'll rebuke, but never in a critical, destructive spirit, and never publicly to shame and punish. That's the godly way. An immature Christian can have a lot of zeal but little wisdom. They can put fire and noise into things that harm rather than help the cause of Christ. I fell into that trap and, like James and John, the Lord rebuked me for judging others.

You see, when we judge we step into the place of God. God alone is the judge of the motives of our hearts. If Jesus had wanted to call down fire on that Samaritan village, He could have done it himself without the help of His disciples. These guys wanted to usurp Jesus' authority, and so He had to set them straight.

I've come to see that my zeal as a disciple—as someone who knows God's Word—has to be directed at *me* first. The inconsistencies and sin I see in the lives of others—and let's face it, you can't help noticing—should remind me to beware of the sin in my own life. Now, if I find myself having to deal with someone else's sin or failure, I'd rather take Paul's advice to heart:

> Brethren, even if a man is caught in any trespass, you who are spiritual, restore such a one in a spirit of gentleness; each one looking to yourself, lest you too be tempted (Galatians 6:1).

Paul knew the Lord's correction is meant to bring restoration in relationship to the Lord and in ministry—not destruction. Restoration takes time, but it's God's goal.

There's another way our critical spirits can harm the body of Christ— when we fight over fine interpretations of the Bible. I've heard people get really nasty with each other—Christian brothers and sisters! Paul says,

> Remind them of these things, and solemnly charge them in the presence of God not to wrangle about words, which is useless, and leads to the ruin of the hearers (2 Timothy 2:14).

When I was a new Christian I spent many useless hours wrangling over words. Added together, those hours probably amount to weeks, even months. I'd argue over anything and everything: When was the rapture going to happen? Can a Christian be possessed by demons? Do you have to be sprinkled or immersed to be truly baptized? Should you be baptized in the name of Jesus only or in the name of the Father, the Son and the Holy Spirit? Some of the arguments produced a lot of heat that looked like zeal for the Lord—but I can't remember any that produced much real light.

In some ways I set myself up for this. After concerts, people came up to me and said, "You know, I don't agree with your position on this or that." I loved it! I'd sit down on the edge of the stage, and a crowd would gather. I'd throw out scriptures, and the other person would lob different ones back at me. We'd have a great time, with our "flesh" exposed for all to see. I didn't realize then that my arguing could cause the ruin of those who listened to me. I was thinking I was a big shot, a spiritual authority, when really I was just a debater with a big ego. I was sharpening a human talent for debate, not a spiritual talent for being quiet, listening and praying.

Paul also said in his warnings to Timothy,

> Avoid worldly and empty chatter, for it will lead to further ungodliness, and their talk will spread like gangrene (2 Timothy 2:16-17).

What a vivid picture. People didn't have the benefit of tetracycline or penicillin in Timothy's day. If you saw a big blue streak going up your arm or leg, you ran to the surgeon and had the infected limb cut off. There was no anesthetic—other than getting drunk or having someone knock you out. Get the idea? This was a drastic and painful condition. So it was the most vivid imagery Paul could use to get his point across. A dispute over words brings out a spirit of contentiousness—and this will spread infection through the body of Christ like gangrene. The only way to remove it is by major and painful surgery.

Why is it important to stay in the right spirit? Because there's a lot more at stake than who's right or wrong—I'm talking about eternal souls.

> The Lord's bond-servant must not be quarrelsome, but be kind to all, able to teach, patient when wronged, with gentleness correcting those who are in opposition, *if perhaps God may grant them repentance leading to the knowledge of the truth, and they may come to their senses and escape from the snare of the devil, having been held captive by him to do his will* (2 Timothy 2:24-26, emphasis added).

Immature Christians mistake a contentious spirit for true zeal. They think they know all the right answers, and that everyone has to see things their way. Paul gave some more strong warnings about this in his letter to Titus:

> Shun foolish controversies and genealogies and strife and disputes about the Law; for they are unprofitable and worthless. Reject a factious man after a first and second warning, knowing that such a man is perverted and is sinning, being self-condemned (Titus 3:9-11).

If we want to grow in Christ, we must ruthlessly evaluate our speech. There's only one standard and one motive acceptable to God. Paul nailed it:

Let no unwholesome word proceed from your mouth, but only such a word as is good for edification according to the need of the moment, that it may give grace to those who hear (Ephesians 4:29).

The last thing I want to say about zeal is more than instruction, it's God's warning to all of us. In Acts 8:9 ff., we read the story of a man named Simon, who practiced magic and sorcery. Everyone in Samaria was astonished by the things he could do, and people called him the "Great Power of God." Then Philip came to town preaching the good news. People began getting saved and baptized. A revival hit, and even

———————◆———————

Do not let your happiness depend on something you may lose...only [upon] the Beloved who will never pass away.

— C. S. Lewis

———————◆———————

Simon was converted. After his conversion he began following Philip around, and saw all the miracles that occurred. Word got back to the other apostles in Jerusalem about what was happening in Samaria, and Peter and John were sent to check things out. They discovered that the new converts had not yet received the baptism of the Spirit, so they began laying their hands on the people and praying for them. Sure enough, the people began receiving the Spirit.

Now when Simon saw that the Spirit was bestowed through the laying on of the apostles' hands, he offered them money, saying, "Give this authority to me as well, so that everyone on whom I lay my hands may receive the Holy Spirit." But Peter said to him, "May your silver perish with you, because you thought you could obtain the gift of God with money!" (Acts 8: 18-20).

Sure, Simon's idea was misguided—but didn't he give up his sorcery business to follow the gospel? Wasn't Peter being a little harsh with him?

I don't think so. Didn't some of us come to the Lord for the wrong motives? We came because we were sick of our lifestyle. Or because we couldn't find peace. Or we needed healing, or our marriage was on the rocks. We came for any number of other reasons.

From New Testament times until today, there have been people who preach the gospel for wrong reasons. They're not following Jesus, they're building their own kingdoms and their own egos. Some people get involved in Christianity simply because it is a market for their merchandise—they can make money. They don't care if people become Christians, they just want to sell their books or records.

Some people start with sincere motives but their appetite for money and fame overcomes them—they continue doing seemingly "good" things, but for all the wrong reasons. They're just putting up a front. They've learned how to effectively fake all the right moves and the right language.

But God will not be mocked. He never lets someone continue in that place for long. They either burn out because it's a work of the flesh, or they are publicly exposed and humiliated—and the name of the Lord gets tarnished in the process.

We always need to check our motives for doing something—even a good thing. And when we are successful in the things of the Lord, we must be careful not to look at the fruit and think it proves we're right with God. Nothing can replace our personal relationship with Him—not even the fruit produced by our ministries.

God wants true disciples who will move beyond selfish motives to a pure motive—and that is to know God himself and the reason He created us. You see, Simon never made that shift. He became interested in the gospel because of what the disciples had to offer—their "tricks" were better than his. They upstaged him. Scripture says that he truly believed in the gospel, but it appears that he never got beyond desiring power so he could have more influence than anyone else.

Simon had zeal all right. He was ready to do whatever it took to get the power he wanted. But his zeal was directed at self-promotion—not at knowing and sharing the love of God.

Working in the music industry, I see this confusion all the time. Today, we see "stars" who become Christians—but they never lay down their music on the altar. They just begin selling Christian versions of their songs. They have lots of zeal—but are they putting it into seeking God? Before I sound like I'm back to the old mode of judging again I have to tell you what I've witnessed. I've seen celebrities come to Christ and get pushed into the spotlight by publishers and record companies before they're ready. When they hit a "pothole," they fall away. Then they say, "Christianity is a joke. It doesn't work." While people looked on and said, "They have so much zeal for God," they were actually using their misdirected zeal to pursue their own interests.

That's what Simon did. The whole time he followed Philip around, he didn't accept the lifestyle of discipleship. He had plenty of zeal to pursue miracles and signs and wonders, but not much interest in pursuing God himself. He had his eyes on the gifts of God, rather than on the God of the gifts.

Paul saw the same kind of misdirected zeal among the Jews. He said,

> For I bear them witness that they have a zeal for God, but not in accordance with knowledge. For not knowing about God's righteousness, and seeking to establish their own, they did not subject themselves to the righteousness of God (Romans 10:2-3).

If Paul looked at your life, would he say the same thing about you? Would he say, "I've got to give you credit, you sure have a lot of zeal for God. You're doing many things in the name of the Lord. But you don't know His righteousness." Are you using your zeal to try to gain something from God, instead of using it as an expression of your gratitude to God for all that He's already done for you?

We can be zealous at keeping rules. We can be zealous debaters and defenders of the truth. We can zealously pursue the gifts of the Spirit. We can even be zealously contentious and fight fleshly battles. But none of this is true zeal for God.

What is zeal for God then? It's giving all our energy and enthusiasm to God's right cause. What does that mean? Jesus made it pretty clear:

> "The foremost [commandment] is, 'Hear, O Israel! The Lord our God is one Lord; and you shall love the Lord your God with all your heart, and with all your soul, and with all your

mind, and with all your strength.' The second is this, 'You shall love your neighbor as yourself.' There is no other commandment greater than these" (Mark 12:29-31).

We are supposed to direct all our zeal into our relationship with the Lord, and then into our relationship with our neighbor. God wants us to get our eyes on Him. Loving Him is to be our cause. He can take care of a lot of other causes without us, but He can't make us love Him with all our heart. That's the work we must do—pursue Him with all our heart and soul and strength.

As David said,

> As the deer pants for the water brooks, so my soul pants for Thee, O God. My soul thirsts for God, for the living God (Psalm 42:1-2).

David was describing true zeal. He thirsted after God. Do you have that kind of desperation? Do you have within that holy fire to know God? God doesn't want to be a casual acquaintance, He wants to be an intimate part of your life—alive and burning at the core of your being.

The second part of the cause we are to advance is to love our neighbor as ourselves. Not correct our neighbor, debate with our neighbor or judge our neighbor, but *love* our neighbor. And how do we love our neighbor? We love them by serving them and doing things that bless them.

> [Christ] gave Himself for us, that He might redeem us from every lawless deed and purify for Himself a people for His own possession, zealous for good deeds (Titus 2:14).

Are we zealous for good deeds? James says, "This is pure and undefiled religion in the sight of our God and Father, to visit orphans and widows in their distress, and to keep oneself unstained by the world" (James 1:27).

Are you zealous for this pure and undefiled religion? Are you self-involved—or are you willing to serve others? The zeal that pleases God is strength and talent directed towards serving others. Jesus reminds His disciples that if we want to be great in the kingdom of God we have to be the servant of all (Matthew 20:26).

Watch out! Our flesh doesn't like the idea of serving others. An attitude of servanthood runs against our egos. Maybe that's why God put so much importance on it. But God doesn't take our flesh into account; He commands us to serve others. The disciple of Christ has no option but to do what He has told us.

I can hear what many of you are thinking: *But we don't need to prove ourselves to God, or to anybody else. He's given us salvation as a gift.*

You're right. But He needs us to turn on our zeal to make salvation real in every area of our lives. He wants us to train ourselves to eagerly serve others in love and compassion.

This is true zeal for God—to know Him and love Him with a deep and consuming love, and to serve others in the same way we would serve Jesus. Anything else is an imitation.

Beware of it.

Jesus said,

"Enter by

the narrow gate…

for…the way

is narrow

that leads to life…"

Matthew 7:13, 14

6

Listen

For The High Call

"When the king came in to look over the dinner guests, he saw there a man not dressed in wedding clothes....Then the king said to the servants, 'Bind him hand and foot, and cast him into the outer darkness; in that place there shall be weeping and gnashing of teeth.' For many are called, but few are chosen" (Matthew 22:11-14).

———————◆———————

It's scary to realize that some people will go before the judgment seat of God convinced they're going to heaven—when they're not. Remember, it's not left to us to judge; it's up to God. But every Christian can benefit by reading and re-reading the parables Jesus taught about the kingdom of heaven, especially the ones that Matthew recorded in his gospel. They're sobering, but they allow the Holy Spirit to do some soul-searching in us.

Today, we're interested in comforting each other. "You just answered an altar call? Said a sinner's prayer? Great, you're in! Now just try to stay out of trouble, will you? Oh, don't be too radical either—you might disturb people."

Jesus had a habit of walking through the countryside, gathering crowds of people around Him and then saying things that were pretty disturbing. Imagine that you've left everything to follow Him—your fishing boat, your tax-collecting booth or your Mom and Dad's beach house on the Sea of Galilee, and then Jesus says,

"Not everyone who says to Me, 'Lord, Lord,' will enter the

kingdom of heaven" (Matthew 7:21).

Remember, Matthew was the guy Jesus called out of a lot of sin and darkness—greed, extorting money from his own countrymen, who knows what else. Even he thought it was important to emphasize this side of Jesus' teaching. Somehow he caught on that it's not enough to answer God's invitation to the wedding feast. And it's not enough to do good Christian deeds—or perform miracles in Jesus' name. He knew that God is after something deeper and stronger.

Why did Jesus relate stories that shook up His most devoted followers? I think about this a lot, because sometimes I find myself getting sloppy about my faith. My Bible can get dusty. I can hear about someone in need and say, "Wow, that's rough...Well, what's on TV tonight?" I can drive past whole neighborhoods—whole cities!—and not worry that most of the people there are in spiritual darkness. I'm thinking, *Well, I'm on my way to the beach, God. Surf's up, you know! Maybe You can get somebody else who's not busy to witness to these people.*

You see, I'm aware of how I confuse God's grace with infinite tolerance. Grace is the fact that He sent us an invitation to His Son's wedding feast at all. Grace is the fact that He purchased all these white robes—with Jesus' blood!—and then hands them out to sinners. Grace is the fact that when Satan comes to devour us God steps in and says, "Back off! This is one of My children. You've got your murderers and liars and thieves and sexual perverts. Keep your hands off My children."

But, brothers and sisters, what is our heart attitude toward all these incredible gifts? When He says, "My Son gave His life so you could be invited to this wedding feast," how do we respond? Do we say, "Okay. He gave His life for me. I'll give my life back to Him"?

We like to run around waving our wedding invitation in people's faces, saying, "Man, look at this! I'm going to the wedding—aren't you?" But then we act like the guy in Jesus' parable. We show up in old, crummy jeans. We hang out in the back of the hall, stuffing ourselves at the buffet table—not acting like guests but more like...Well, I better not say that. Somebody will get their feelings hurt.

That's the problem I'm getting at. So much of our Christianity is based on wanting to feel good. "Come to Jesus, because it's a better 'high' than drugs!" "Come, and be blessed!" "The party's on!" We keep on our breakfast tables little plastic boxes of promise cards, filled with all the neat, sweet things about God. Yeah, they're all true. Every single one.

But there's another side to God, a side we'll all have to face some day. I'd rather preach the neat and sweet stuff, believe me. People call you controversial when you tell them the hard stuff. I'd rather be a comforter. But the fact is, we're all going to experience God as our righteous judge. Don't be lulled to sleep, thinking you can ignore God's commands because, after all, He knows what a rough life you had before you were a Christian. He comforts—but He comforts us with His grace so that we can grow in spiritual strength to do His will on earth. So God is gentle—and at the same time He is a righteous judge.

What will you answer when He asks, "What did you do with all the grace I poured out on you? Did you do my will?"

Let's look at this, because we can become confused about God's love and grace, and His righteous judgment.

First, it's true that the invitation into God's family is offered freely to everyone. John 3:16, probably the most well-known verse in the Bible, tells us so. But like the man who came to the wedding in the wrong clothes, many people who call themselves Christians mistake God's *invitation* for His complete *approval*.

Let's get even more basic. God did not create anyone for the purpose of destroying them. I've never met anyone who planted a tree in their yard for firewood. For shade, yes, or for fruit. But not just for firewood. Only when the tree becomes unfruitful or dies is it cut down and burned. God has invited us all to live with Him in eternity. But that doesn't mean we can say to ourselves, "God is merciful. If I'm still disobedient when I get there, it won't matter. I can just wave my invitation in God's face." According to Jesus, that won't work. God will judge us according to what we did with the free righteousness He offered. Do you think He'd pour out the blood of His only Son just to have us trample it?

Preachers often make the judgment seat of Christ sound like a giant charity giveaway. But having an invitation is not enough. There's an RSVP on the invitation to eternal life. We have to respond to it. By our lives, we let the Lord know we're serious about accepting His invitation.

We love to quote God's invitation, don't we? After all, Jesus said it.

> "For God so loved the world, that He gave His only begotten Son, that whoever believes in Him should not perish, but have eternal life" (John 3:16).

59

But the word *believe* doesn't mean we go around saying, "I believe. I believe. Praise God, I believe." Even the demons believe in God that way. No. Our belief has to be much stronger than that. The Greek word Jesus used is *pisteuo*. It means to "adhere to," to "have faith in," to "commit to." It means proving that we believe by the way we live.

That's how we accept Christ's invitation—by clothing ourselves in a new way of living. Changing our spiritual robes—taking off our old life and putting on the new life.

The New Testament clearly outlines some things that become part of our new life in Christ. It's these things that show we've come into real heart-union with Christ. It's the proof we've come for the wedding with Him.

Jesus was clear about the first point I want to discuss:

> "Everyone therefore who shall confess Me before men, I will also confess him before My Father who is in heaven. But whoever shall deny Me before men, I will also deny him before My Father who is in heaven" (Matthew 10:32–33).

We don't find this promise in many promise boxes: If we deny Him, He'll deny us. Anyone who isn't comfortable standing up for Christ here on earth will be very uncomfortable at the judgment. Because Christ will not stand up for us there.

This was Paul's testimony:

> For I am not ashamed of the gospel, for it is the power of God for salvation to everyone who believes (Romans 1:16).

Paul was the kind of committed, sold-out believer that Jesus looked for. He had no reason to be ashamed of Christ or the gospel. Paul was so flat-out amazed at God's grace—because he had worked so hard as a Pharisee to *earn* His favor. Once he understood the invitation—to the biggest "social event" in the universe—he couldn't keep it to himself. It captivated him. He called himself a "captive of Christ" long after Jesus said, "I call you friends."

So why is it we say we have God's invitation, but then act ashamed of it—too embarrassed to tell our friends? What does that say about our belief? It doesn't sound like the same kind of believing Paul practiced, does it? If we're ashamed to own Christ publicly, what can we expect at the final judgment?

Jesus always taught that sharing our faith with others is a fruit of the Christian life. His last word to us before He left the earth was a command to go into all the world and share the gospel with everyone. Is this fruit in your life—are you free to actively proclaim Christ? Or are you too ashamed of your behavior to tell others you're a Christian? Worse, are you ashamed of Him?

Jesus was clear on another fruit that shows itself in the life of a true disciple. There's a passage in Matthew I can't get away from. Sometimes we like to skip it. *Read it:*

> "Then the King will say to those on His right, 'Come, you who are blessed of My Father, inherit the kingdom prepared for you from the foundation of the world. For I was hungry, and you gave Me something to eat; I was thirsty, and you gave Me drink; I was a stranger, and you invited Me in; naked, and you clothed Me; I was sick, and you visited Me; I was in prison, and you came to Me.' Then the righteous will answer Him, saying, 'Lord when did we see You hungry, and feed You, or thirsty, and give You drink? And when did we see You a stranger, and invite You in, or naked, and clothe You? And when did we see You sick, or in prison, and come to You?' And the King will answer and say to them, 'Truly I say to you, to the extent that you did it to one of these brothers of Mine, even the least of them, you did it to Me'" (Matthew 25:34-40).

Oh, Father, let your Spirit burn these words into our hearts.

In this story, Jesus said the righteous are those who take off the old life of self-centeredness and put on the new life of loving and serving others. They're the ones who feed the hungry and clothe the naked. They visit the prisoners, and welcome strangers. No, we're not *saved* by doing good works. But if we are saved, our lives will produce the fruit of good works. We'll have a new heart within—a new way of looking at people. Our new heart will compel us to reach out to others. Like Paul, we'll be captivated—wanting to bless them as we've been blessed.

If you can see people in real need and not feel any urge to help them, you have to ask yourself, Is Jesus really living in me?

John said,

> Whoever has the world's goods, and beholds his brother in need and closes his heart against him, how does the love of God abide in him? Little children, let us not love with word or with tongue, but in deed and truth. We shall know by this that we are of the truth, and shall assure our heart before Him (1 John 3:17-19).

And Paul says,

> Do you think lightly of the riches of His kindness and forbearance and patience, not knowing that the kindness of God leads you to repentance? But because of your stubbornness and unrepentant heart you are storing up wrath for yourself in the day of wrath and revelation of the righteous judgement of God, who will render to every man according to his deeds (Romans 2:4-6).

God will judge us in righteousness. He'll judge us according to what we have done. And then He will reward us. If we've done good works out of a pure love for Jesus, we'll inherit eternal life. If we've done anything less—or if we acted out of wrong motives—then we will not inherit eternal life.

There will be a lot of surprised people at the final judgment. The Father will look at them and ask, "Who are you?" And they'll say, "C'mon Lord. You know us. We did lots of incredible things in Your name. We said to demons, 'Demon power, we cast you out in the name of Jesus.' And they left. In Your name we prophesied, proclaiming the Word of God. And now You're saying You don't recognize us? There must be some mistake!" And the Father will say, "Sorry, I never knew you. It's too late. Leave my presence forever."

There have been times when I've doubted whether I was saved. I have thought, *Maybe I am not really a Christian. Maybe I'm only fooling myself. What if I get to the judgment of God and He says, "Sorry, I never knew you."*

How can we know that won't be the case? The answer is found in

1 John 3:18-19. It says that if we serve Jesus by serving others, we have confidence that we're going to heaven. When we serve out of compassion and obedience—when we speak the gospel and live the gospel—we have within us the guarantee that we are saved. When I doubt my salvation, I look at the things the love of God motivates me to do. I look at all the ways I am different now from the way I used to be. I know God is at work in my life—because I can't make myself kind, generous or patient. I know that when those things are present in my life, it's because I have Jesus, the fruit-producer, living inside me. That's what gives me confidence to go on.

Some of you may be wondering what I'm getting at. I started out by talking about a spiritual "wedding feast" and ended up talking about our lives producing fruit. It's clear that salvation can't be earned, but at the

———————◆———————

Christ was the greatest Victim this side of the Cross, but the greatest Victor on the other; and the daily path was the way of the Cross: every selfish motive and every selfish thought was at once dealt with by the Holy Spirit.

—Rees Howells

———————◆———————

same time, Jesus, Paul and the other apostles all talked about producing good fruit. A lot of people get confused and start pushing other Christians around, telling them they're not saved because they missed a chance to witness to somebody. Or because they were going through a hard time, and missed an opportunity to serve. It's not our business—it's never our business to judge who's in and who's out.

But it is our job to remind each other to change our clothes before the wedding. I can't judge you, but I have to remind you. And you have to keep reminding me—"Keith, how's your heart? Have you gotten hard, or lazy? Are you making the mistake of saying, 'I accepted Jesus some time ago. I used to lead a Bible study. I led some people to the Lord back then.

That's proof enough of my righteousness, isn't it?'"

Man, it's so easy to forget that I'm supposed to be changing all along the way. This is a tricky area theologically—and some people preach that you can lose your salvation. All I'm saying is that it's much safer to live close to Jesus, so we know we're becoming more like Him every hour, every day. It's not such a bad thing to strive to serve God better, more from the heart. It's not so terrible to keep His righteous-judge side in mind.

It seems clear that when we stand before God, Jesus wants us to be covered in His robe of righteousness, not just waving our invitation.

It's hard to understand why in the parable of the wedding feast the king was so harsh to the one guest—unless we understand this point. In the time between when the invitation was given and the time the guests sat down with the king's son to celebrate, they were supposed to change their clothes. They were invited to the wedding feast in the clothes they were wearing, but they weren't supposed to show up to the feast in them.

If you were invited to a friend's wedding and you knew it was going to be a dress-up deal—formal dresses and tuxes—you wouldn't show up sweaty and dirty in your ditch-digging clothes. If you did, it would show your real heart-attitude towards your friend: "Sorry—I knew your wedding was today, but my own work was more important than getting ready to honor you."

This is the point. God has invited us to feast with Him and His son, Jesus. The invitation, with your name on it, was written in blood while you were still wearing your sin, your rebellion and your faithlessness. Do we see what an honor it is to be invited into God's presence? Are we changed in our hearts because of it—do we let ourselves become robed in righteousness because we're so humbled, so thankful to be asked to come at all?

Accepting an invitation means that we understand the place of welcome and honor that's offered to us. And we show our gratitude by dressing appropriately for the occasion. Standing before God is not a come-as-you-are affair. Only one set of clothes is acceptable—the robes of righteousness.

And where do we get these robes? Isaiah said,

> I will rejoice greatly in the Lord, my soul will exult in my
> God; for He has clothed me with garments of salvation, He

has wrapped me with a robe of righteousness (Isaiah 61:10).

God provides the clothes we need for the feast. That's grace. We have no righteousness outside of Jesus Christ. We have no way to stand before God and be accepted on our own merit. We must throw ourselves on His grace, and ask Him to change us and clothe us in His righteousness. And He will.

Paul said,

> For if by the transgression of the one, death reigned through the one, much more those who receive the abundance of grace and of the gift of righteousness will reign in life through the One, Jesus Christ (Romans 5:17).

God offers us His nature and asks us to take it on as our nature—in place of our old nature. First, we become righteous because He is righteous. Then His righteousness is worked into our hearts. The process originates with God, but we have to take what He gives us—righteousness, grace—and let more of it grow in our lives. More righteousness. More grace. When God shows us mercy, He looks to see if we are showing mercy to others. And if we don't show mercy, it demonstrates that we don't honor or respect the robe of mercy He offers us. So in that way, mercy is taken away from us—because *we* threw it in the mud!

> "For whoever has, to him shall more be given, and he shall have an abundance; but whoever does not have, even what he has shall be taken away from him" (Matthew 13:12).

Take some time to think about all this. It's a serious matter.

Jesus ended the parable of the wedding feast with the words, "Many are called but few are chosen." The invitation to the marriage feast of the Lamb has gone out to everyone who has ever lived. We're all *invited* because of the grace of God. But we're *chosen* to be a part of that feast by what we do with that grace. It's a paradox that makes sense when you realize God wants changed lives.

Paul knew this when he wrote,

> ...work out your salvation with fear and trembling; for it is

God who is at work in you, both to will and to work for His good pleasure (Philippians 2:12-13).

When we really enter into the righteousness of Jesus, we are changed. Then, when we get to the wedding, it will be easy for God and everyone else to see that we took the invitation seriously. We honored and respected God enough to come dressed in wedding clothes and ready for the party.

"Let us rejoice and be glad and give the glory to Him, for the marriage of the Lamb has come and His bride has made herself ready." And it was given to her to clothe herself in fine linen, bright and clean; for the fine linen is the righteous acts of the saints. And he said to me, "Write, 'Blessed are those who are invited to the marriage supper of the Lamb'" (Revelation 19:7-9).

Jesus prayed,

"My Father,
if it is possible,
let this cup pass from Me;
yet not as I will,
but as Thou wilt."

Matthew 26:39

Accept
Suffering And Trials

For momentary, light affliction is producing for us an eternal weight of glory far beyond all comparison (2 Corinthians 4:17).

———————◆———————

A friend once said to me, "Even if there were no heaven or hell, I'd follow Jesus—because being a Christian is the most exciting and fun life you can lead. God gives me everything I need. Hallelujah!"

This friend is like others I meet—Christians who see God as a big "Sugar Daddy in the Sky." They think God works 24-hours-a-day to make life smooth for us—to shelter us from anything painful or stressful, and to give us everything we want.

How does this attitude compare with the life of servanthood and suffering that Jesus led? How does it compare with the lives of Jesus' true disciples?

Oh, we love the way the Gospels show us the power of Christ's life, but we don't want to follow Him in the way He lived. Blessings—sure. But are we willing—and prepared—to follow Christ in His obedience to God, even if God chooses to lead us through suffering? We don't want to hear God's Word unless it appeals to our flesh, blesses us and makes life more pleasant for us.

We talk a lot about being God's end-time generation. Maybe we're just a generation of overindulged, take-the-easy-way Christians.

Jesus' ultimate example of obedience was His willingness to deny what His flesh wanted and go to the cross to finish the will of God. We hear how He was scourged and beaten by the Roman soldiers. How He hung in agony on the cross. It makes us sad, but we're grateful that He suffered, because His pain brought about our salvation. His suffering freed us from the load of sin and guilt we were carrying, and gave us a new start. But was that the end of it?

Paul tells the Philippians:

> For to you it has been granted for Christ's sake, not only to believe in Him, but also to suffer for His sake (Philippians 1:29).

Wait a minute—God has *granted* us to suffer? Like it's some kind of favor? Because this goes against what most of us believe about God, we immediately begin to rationalize. We say to ourselves, *There's no need for a Christian to suffer today. Jesus suffered on the cross to give us abundant life. He suffered "once and for all" so that none of us will have to feel sad, get sick or be mocked.*

What we've done is change the gospel. We've taken the good news that God has created a way of salvation, and made it into a "gos-pill"! We've created a wonder cure that takes away all our aches and pains. We promise people that all their material needs and ninety-five percent of their wants will be taken care of. If the gospel promised a joyride through life, wouldn't everyone want to be a Christian?

When trouble comes along, what do we do? We rebuke it and stand against it in the name of Jesus. Then we wonder why God let us down when the trial doesn't instantly vanish. We treat prayer like a spray-on window cleaner.

But Paul talks about suffering in a way that makes me think he knew a secret we've forgotten. What did he know about God's eternal purposes in suffering that we choose to ignore?

First, many scriptures in the New Testament tell us we will suffer with Jesus. Paul explains to the Corinthians:

> Therefore I am well content with weaknesses, with insults, with distresses, with persecutions, with difficulties, for Christ's sake; for when I am weak, then I am strong (2 Corinthians 12:10).

What?! Paul is "well content" with all this terrible stuff happening to him? He wasn't content because God blessed him with a late-model chariot. Or because of his home improvements, or his seminar curriculum or his career advancement. Paul was content with things we avoid like the plague: difficulties, persecutions, distresses, insults. How many of us would be content after going through what Paul did? How many of us would survive this kind of ordeal with our faith intact?

Paul forced himself to face the challenge of suffering, like a man charging through the gates of hell. He pushed himself, like a runner, to endure the pain, always keeping his eye on the prize.

If we want to be true disciples who know how to endure, we have to understand the secret of Paul's contentment. What was it?

Paul understood that God had orchestrated whatever circumstances he found himself in. He knew that suffering wasn't due to meaningless accidents. Listen to this:

> Rejoice always; pray without ceasing; in everything give thanks; for this is God's will for you in Christ Jesus (1 Thessalonians 5:16–18).

Paul knew there was warfare going on—a spiritual resistance. Paul reminded Timothy that, as a result of that resistance, he had suffered persecution while trying to help the young churches. Then Paul warned us: anyone who desires to live godly in Christ Jesus *will be persecuted* (2 Timothy 3:12). Paul also warned his young friend not to be ashamed of the testimony of the Lord—that Jesus died a criminal's death, as an outcast. He told Timothy to join him in suffering for the gospel (2 Timothy 1:8-9). Because Paul understood God's purposes, he told the Colossians that he actually rejoiced in his suffering (Colossians 1:24). He even sang in prison with a bloody back. Do *we* understand the purposes of suffering? Are we able to rejoice in our trials, like Paul?

The Bible lists at least eight of God's purposes for hardship in our lives.

Primarily, God allows us to suffer because He knows what suffering will build in us. If we accept Christ as our Lord we must also accept that He will mold us into people who radiate the fruit of the Spirit.

> It is God who is at work in you, both to will and to work for His good pleasure (Philippians 2:13).

James tells us that God works His good pleasure in us—not by blessing us with goodies, but by sending trials and persecution.

> Consider it all joy, my brethren, when you encounter various trials, knowing that the testing of your faith produces *endurance*. And let endurance have its perfect result, that you may be perfect and complete, lacking in nothing (James 1:2–4, emphasis added).

God can build godly qualities in our lives, if only we'd realize that suffering is one of the major tools He uses to do this. Sometimes we even stop blaming the demons for our troubles, and begin to murmur about God. We forget that our Lord was a *carpenter*. He wants to chisel away our rough edges and create something beautiful. But the minute things start getting tough, we complain—"God, this hurts too much!" We try to detour the Holy Spirit from His work. God asks us, "Do you love me?" We say, "Yes." Then God asks, "Do you *trust* me?" And we say, "Well, yes, of course—but you're not going to work on my selfishness or greed, are you? Why not teach me how to be a gracious and humble *rich person* instead?"

And, we limp along with the same old sins, year after year. We won't forgive somebody for what they did to us in the past. We can't figure out why we're full of bitterness—so God sends more trials, to reveal our bitter heart. But we cry and pray, "I rebuke this suffering, in Jesus' name." Again and again God brings us back to our hidden sin. He wants to reveal the "old man" to us, so that we can let him die, and then come alive in God. He wants us to say, "God, I don't care anymore. I want your life and your healing more than I want my own way. I'll lie still and endure this." When we release ourselves to Him, He's able to finish the job quickly.

> And not only this, but we also exult in our tribulations, knowing that tribulation brings about perseverance; and perseverance, proven character; and proven character, hope; and hope does not disappoint, because the love of God has been poured out within our hearts through the Holy Spirit who was given to us (Romans 5:3-5).

If we learn to ask God what He's working into us, our outward trials begin to produce godly qualities within. We say we want to be people of endurance, character, love and hope. Paul says we get those things by taking hold of suffering and pressing through our trials with joy and faith. So God takes us at our word and uses His chisel of trials to build these qualities into our lives.

Do you realize Paul considered it a privilege and an honor to suffer with Christ? Today, most of us would say, "Man, that's sick, isn't it?" That just shows how far *off* our understanding is of spiritual wisdom. Paul gave a second reason why God allows suffering:

> The Spirit Himself bears witness with our spirit that we are children of God, and if children, heirs also, heirs of God and fellow heirs with Christ, if indeed we suffer with Him in order that we may also be glorified with Him (Romans 8:16-17).

Do you want be glorified with Jesus? Then live as He lived, and be crucified—spiritually speaking—as He was crucified.

Some people think that Christ's suffering means only His death on the cross. But Jesus suffered through His whole life on earth. He watched men and women live sinful and wicked lives, though He created us to be spotless and blameless. Then He had to deal with his disciples' constant lack of faith. Imagine repeating the same simple message over and over, almost despairing that even His own disciples would ever understand.

> And Jesus…said, "O unbelieving and perverted generation, how long shall I be with you? How long shall I put up with you?" (Matthew 17:17).

Jesus cares for His creation, and grieves when we continually miss the mark. He's like a mom and dad watching the child they raised so lovingly get into drugs or something else destructive. We're like the rebellious child who says, "It's none of my parents' business. Why should they care? It's my life!" Parents can't help but care, and because they care they suffer. That's why Jesus suffers when we turn our backs on Him and go our own way.

Do we suffer with Jesus in this way, grieving over the lost humanity all around us? Grieving over our own failures?

Jesus also suffered the rejection of His family. His own brothers didn't even believe in Him (John 7:5). He wasn't recognized by His own people. "He came to His own, and those who were His own did not receive Him" (John 1:11). The Pharisees accused Him and plotted to kill Him (John 7:1; John 11:47-57). He was slandered and called an agent of Satan because He healed people. (Matthew 12:22-29). Talk about being misunderstood.

As Jesus' disciples watched Him go through all this, Jesus told them plainly that they could expect the same.

> "A disciple is not above his teacher, nor a slave above his master. It is enough for the disciple that he become as his teacher, and the slave as his master. If they have called the head of the house Beelzebul, how much more the members of his household!" (Matthew 10:24-25).

Let's face it, if we are called Christians—followers of Christ—we have to follow Him through the temptations and challenges in this world. And we need to follow His example in how we respond.

> For you have been called for this purpose, since Christ also suffered for you, leaving you an example for you to follow in His steps, who committed no sin, nor was any deceit found in His mouth; and while being reviled, He did not revile in return; while suffering, He uttered no threats, but kept entrusting Himself to Him who judges righteously (1 Peter 2:21-23).

You may be thinking, *Okay, Keith. That's enough about suffering. Don't get too heavy about this.* But I'll bet few of us have heard many messages on this subject. So bear with me.

When the U.S. Army recruits soldiers they don't say, "Come, and suffer hardship. We'll grind you to a pulp—so you can 'be all that you can be.'" They never tell you *before* officer training school that you're going to be harassed and overworked and pushed to the extreme—by your own people!—before they approve you to the rank of officer. They soft-sell it, make it look glamorous and exciting. Sweat and blood and dirt don't *sell.* That's the way most of our preaching is too. "Heavens! Don't tell people they're going to have to *suffer* to be what God wants them to be. Tell them the glory cloud will carry them away."

I think Paul would have been upset, after all he went through, hearing all our sales-oriented, false promises. He told us straight:

> Suffer hardship with me, as a good soldier of Christ Jesus (2 Timothy 2:3).

What do we do? We want to live out our faith as though we're lying on a big overstuffed mattress. We want to lie back on a "posturepedic cross" and take it easy. No one can tell we're Christians except for our

---◆---

Your path, with its unexplained...turmoil, and mine with its [pain]...they are His paths, on which He will show himself faithful.
—Amy Carmichael

---◆---

bumper stickers and our coffee mugs. But the way I read my Bible, things are going to change. God is going to bring some real hell on earth, and it will separate the sheep from the goats—the true Christian from the pew-warmer.

The third reason God allows suffering and adversity is to make us battle ready. He wants us to be trained for the spiritual battles ahead, whatever form they may take in our lives.

We were talking about soldiers earlier. Before soldiers go to war, they are put through training that's like hell on earth. Why? Because the government wants to be mean? No. Because they want new recruits to know how to avoid getting killed when they get to the battlefield! God knows there's a battle for every Christian in every generation. He knows how fierce it's going to be. And He knows how much we need to be trained to fight. He'll use hard circumstances to train us for the times we live in. If we resist His training, we're going to be in big trouble when the real battles come.

The fourth reason God allows us to suffer is to force us to *rely on Jesus* and not on our own strength.

> There was given me a thorn in the flesh, a messenger of Satan to buffet me—to keep me from exalting myself! Concerning this I entreated the Lord three times that it might depart from me. And He has said to me, "My grace is sufficient for you, for power is perfected in weakness" (2 Corinthians 12:7-9).

Paul understood—with spiritual understanding—that when he was the weakest, when the most impossible odds were against him, then he could be the strongest. Why? Because hard circumstances forced him back to God.

Do you want to know Jesus better? How do you think that's going to happen? You see, Jesus *himself* is our way of escape as we go through difficulty. "I can do all things through Him who strengthens me," Paul said (Philippians 4:13). We lean on Jesus Christ for the power to make it through hard times. Without the hard times there is little reason for most of us to lean into Jesus. So His power is made perfect in us when we're at our weakest. Then we have the chance to stop living in our own strength and admit that we can't go on alone.

It's so simple. But many of us miss the point and struggle on—sometimes for years—in our own strength. We're frustrated, ineffective and powerless. Finally, we cry out to God, "Okay—*You* give me the strength!" And that's what He wanted to hear all along.

The next major reason God allows us to suffer is that suffering conforms us to the image of Jesus.

> But we have this treasure in earthen vessels, *that the surpassing greatness of the power may be of God and not from ourselves;* we are afflicted in every way, but not crushed; perplexed, but not despairing; persecuted, but not forsaken; struck down, but not destroyed; always carrying about in the body the dying of Jesus, *that the life of Jesus also may be manifested in our body.* For we who live are constantly being delivered over to death for

Jesus' sake, *that the life of Jesus also may be manifested in our mortal flesh* (2 Corinthians 4:7-11, emphasis added).

Trials and suffering push us until we come to the end of our strength. Then we die to ourselves, and allow Jesus to live through us. We all say we want more of Jesus and less of us, don't we? Are we willing to go through whatever it takes to let that happen?

A sixth reason God allows us to suffer is that it helps us develop compassion for others.

When we experience problems and struggles, we're able to identify with people who are suffering. One reason Jesus became a man was so that He could identify with us. Paul talked about this in his letter to the Corinthians. And we read about it in Hebrews, too:

Blessed be the God and Father of our Lord Jesus Christ, the Father of mercies and God of all comfort; who comforts us in all our affliction *so that we may be able to comfort those who are in any affliction with the comfort with which we ourselves are comforted by God.* For just as the sufferings of Christ are ours in abundance, so also our comfort is abundant through Christ (2 Corinthians 1:3-5, emphasis added).

Therefore, [Jesus] had to be made like His brethren in all things, that He might become a merciful and faithful high priest in things pertaining to God, to make propitiation for the sins of the people. For since He Himself was tempted in that which He has suffered, He is able to come to the aid of those who are tempted (Hebrews 2:17-18).

This is the *abundant life* that we're entitled to in Christ—the suffering of Christ in abundance! Can I hear a "hallelujah" on that? But the good news is that through our abundance of suffering we can know the abundance of the Father's comfort. And when we receive His comfort, we can comfort others who are afflicted. But if we've never needed to be comforted ourselves, then we have nothing to offer to a dying world.

Next, the Bible teaches that God allows us to suffer to help us take our eyes off this world—which isn't our final home anyway—and fix our hearts on the eternal joy set before us.

Therefore, since we have so great a cloud of witnesses sur-rounding us, let us also lay aside every encumbrance, and the sin which so easily entangles us, and let us run with endurance the race that is set before us, fixing our eyes on Jesus, the author and perfecter of faith, who for the joy set before Him endured the cross, despising the shame, and has sat down at the right hand of the throne of God (Hebrews 12:1-2).

In one way, earth is a training ground for Christians. The experiences we go through are meant to prepare us for our heavenly reward. This theme is repeated over and over in the New Testament. Jesus said,

"Blessed are you when men cast insults at you, and persecute you, and say all kinds of evil against you falsely, on account of Me. Rejoice, and be glad, for your reward in heaven is great, for so they persecuted the prophets who were before you" (Matthew 5:11-12).

James said,

Blessed is a man who perseveres under trial; for once he has been approved, he will receive the crown of life, which the Lord has promised to those who love Him (James 1:12).

And Paul said,

Therefore we do not lose heart....For momentary, light afflic-tion is producing for us an eternal weight of glory far beyond all comparison, while we look not at the things which are seen, but at the things which are not seen; for the things which are seen are temporal, but the things which are not seen are eternal (2 Corinthians 4:16-18).

These Scriptures challenge those of us who want to be disciples of Jesus because of the earthly benefits we expect. There are no promises of riches or a pain-free life here. As Paul looked back over his life he wrote,

"If we have hoped in Christ in this life only, we are of all men most to be pitied" (1 Corinthians 15:19). Why did he say this? Because without Christ's resurrection—and our future with Him in a glorious eternity—our struggles wouldn't have much purpose.

But we know there is an eternity with Christ to come, and that there will be a final judgment. And God will reward those who allowed Him to build His character into them through hardship.

In light of all this we have to make our decisions here on earth. We have to resist those things that are easy to give in to. We stand firm when tempted to follow after the lusts of our flesh. We endure suffering because our reward is in heaven, not down here. Here is where we go to war. And after we've been to war, then we go home for the victory party.

Finally, the Bible teaches that God allows suffering as a seal upon our lives.

> "My son, do not regard lightly the discipline of the Lord, nor faint when you are reproved by Him; for those whom the Lord loves He disciplines, and He scourges every son whom He receives." It is for discipline that you endure; God deals with you as with sons; for what son is there whom his father does not discipline?…All discipline for the moment seems not to be joyful, but sorrowful; yet to those who have been trained by it, afterwards it yields the peaceful fruit of righteousness (Hebrews 12:5-11).

Difficulties and trials are a seal of our acceptance as children of God. In Hebrews we are told that because God loves us, He takes the time to correct us. So in the end, it's the discipline and chastening from the Lord that prepares us to enter into the Kingdom of God.

Do you know how Paul encouraged his converts, how he cheered them up?

> And after they had preached the gospel to that city and had made many disciples, they returned to Lystra and to Iconium and to Antioch, strengthening the souls of the disciples, encouraging them to continue in the faith, and saying, "Through many tribulations we must enter the kingdom of God" (Acts 14:21–22).

That's what Paul did to strengthen and encourage the disciples. He told them that they'd enter the kingdom through many tribulations. Tribulations—as in *trials, hardships, disappointments, heartaches* and *rejection.* Is that an encouraging word for Christians today?

If I said to you, "I want to encourage you; I want to strengthen you; I see many trials ahead for you," I don't think you'd be encouraged at all. You'd probably think, "God has forsaken me. Where are my blessings? I'm cursed." There are many things we don't want to hear in the church today. We don't want to hear anything that upsets us, makes us uncomfortable or shakes our self-centered, self-sufficient lives.

The attitude of the early church was as different from that of today's church as night is from day. They saw trials as a wonderful time of training for the Lord. We look at them as an infringement on our lives. Too often, we attribute God's work in our lives to the devil, because what God is doing hurts. And we have false prophets who prophesy that God wants us to enjoy outward peace and prosperity. But the Bible tells us we will have inner peace and outer turmoil.

We're children and heirs of God *if* we suffer with Him. We don't need to make ourselves suffer, but when we're obedient to the Word of the Lord, we will endure adversity. When we do the things God says we should do—when we speak out when He tells us to—we *will* suffer.

Suffering is a blessing; Scripture says so.

I think God wants more disciples like Paul. Paul embraced suffering and went forward in the Lord's strength, reaping the internal benefits of its work in his life—peace, joy, inner freedom. He knew the purpose of suffering in his life.

That was Paul's secret, and it needs to become our secret, too.

Jesus said,

"...*Ten virgins*

...*took their lamps,*

and went out

to meet

the bridegroom.

Five of them

were foolish

...*and took no oil*

with them."

Matthew 25:1-3

8
Shine
With God's Light

"You are the light of the world. A city set on a hill cannot be hidden....Let your light shine before men in such a way that they may see your good works, and glorify your Father who is in heaven" (Matthew 5:14, 16).

◆

Jesus used some vivid images to show His disciples what they should be like. He said we were to be the light of the world, a city set on a hill, the salt of the earth (Matthew 5:13). Jesus wants us to know that God expects us to be human expressions of Him for the sake of others.

A light is something others see. A city set on a hill gives others direction. Salt is something others taste.

Jesus said His followers would be the visible, smellable, touchable, tasteable expression of God to others. He warned us to be careful not to let the light of our faith go out, like the five foolish virgins in the parable (Matthew 25:1-3). In every way we are to be growing, living reflections of God so that others are drawn to Him. Not to us, to Him. That's what Jesus had in mind for His disciples then, and He expects no less from His disciples today.

Do people look at you and the way you live and see Jesus? Most of the people around us are not going to sit down and read the Bible, even if you give them one. The only Jesus they see is the Jesus that lives in us.

Paul told the Corinthians:

> You are our letter, written in our hearts, known and read by all men; being manifested that you are a letter of

Christ, cared for by us, written not with ink, but with the Spirit of the living God, not on tablets of stone, but on tablets of human hearts (2 Corinthians 3:2-3).

How we live each day is more important than we realize. No matter what we do, our actions either draw people closer to Jesus, or push them further away from Him. Do we take it seriously when God says we're His "open letter" to the world? Do we dare to continue living in a way that gives a distorted reflection of Him? If we're serious about loving God and doing His will, then we have to do whatever is necessary to get our lives in order—and that means aligning ourselves to the Word of God. That's the only sure way we can present a clear picture of God. Paul writes to the Ephesians, "Be imitators of God, as beloved children" (Ephesians 5:1).

Why? Because when we imitate the character of God, others are attracted to what they see in us.

How do we imitate Him? By imitating His faithfulness to people, His integrity and His impartial love for every person. When we do this, we become the salt and light of the world.

Being an open letter to our world makes me think of Richard Gene Lowe. When Melody and I met him, Richard was eighty-four years old, and had served the Lord for seventy of those years.

He lived in a little one-room apartment filled with piles of clutter. He was never there to clean it because he was always out helping others. Richard was one of the first Christians we met, and the love and zeal he had for Jesus helped convince us that God was real—and that He was really worth serving. Richard was a radiant example of God's goodness. Even though he was poor he was always willing to reach out to others in need. He volunteered for many years at some evangelistic healing services in town, working to help the people who came in wheelchairs. He saw many of them leave without those chairs, too. He had amazing stories of God's supernatural healings—his own and others. He really built our faith.

Richard spent hours with us and our friends telling us about Jesus—how to talk to Him, how to worship Him, how to love Him. He would hang out in our van with Melody and me as we did our errands or went to garage sales. And all he talked about was Jesus.

Even though Richard had hardly any money—he wore a five-dollar second-hand suit—he bought clothing at thrift stores and gave it to people who were more needy. Richard didn't have a lot of material things, but he freely gave what he had—time and love—for the glory of the Lord and the blessing of others. Richard is with the Lord now, but I have a feeling he'll be one of the first people to greet me and show me around when I get to heaven.

Richard was faithful to God, and God was faithful to him.

But what does it mean that God is faithful? As Paul said,

> ...[even] if we are faithless, He remains faithful; for He cannot deny Himself (2 Timothy 2:13).

*Even if we are faithless, God remains faithful....*Faithfulness isn't a quality God puts on and takes off on a whim. It's like His love and His holiness—He *is* love. He *is* holy. And He *is* faithful.

How different we are from God. If someone hurts us, we look for a way to strike back. Right? Revenge! If our friends gossip about us, we gossip about them. If someone hurts us we think we have a right to do the same.

God's message to us is "You can walk away from me, ignore me or misrepresent me—but I'm not going to break my promise to you. I'll keep loving you and giving you chances right down to the finish line. I'm not going to break my promise to you because you broke your promise to me. If in the end you don't choose to return to me, then we'll both live with the consequences of your choice. But don't expect me to come down to your level. I cannot be unfaithful. It's not my nature. I don't have a bailout plan if you break faith with me. I will continue on regardless."

This is amazing! Do you see it? God is faithful and will not break faith with us. He is light, as John said, and there is no darkness in Him (1 John 1:5).

When He says, "I'll be faithful," He isn't keeping some secret clause buried in fine print in the contract. It's all *on the table*. In plain view. And John warns us that if we say we're like Him but keep a little unfaithfulness tucked away in the dark, we're only lying to ourselves—and to God. And we're misrepresenting ourselves to the world. We're not being "light" to them.

Do you see why God places such a high value on faithfulness to Him? He wants to know if we'll really be His hands and feet to the people around us who live in darkness. And if we're not faithful, then we should beg God to teach us faithfulness. Beg Him to burn faithfulness into our character. People need to see the faithfulness of God in our faithfulness—to Him and to them.

Faithfulness means consistency. God can be counted on—He's not our friend one day and our enemy the next. He's loving, kind, gracious and compassionate. He demonstrated these attributes in Genesis, and He continues to demonstrate them today. God hasn't changed with the times.

How about you? Are you consistent? Can people rely on you? Can you be counted on when things are going well and when they're not? Or do you hide your Christian behavior depending on who you're with? Does your faith go up and down with the balance in your bank account? How do you react to God when your kids are sick? Does your love for God change according to your circumstances?

God wants us to be consistent in our love for Him regardless of our circumstances.

And what about your faithfulness to those in your church? Do you only go to church when you feel like it? Do you make pledges to support missionaries or ministries when things are going well, and then back out when you see a new car you want? Can your friends count on your help when there's hard work to be done? Sometimes we're quick to make commitments with our mouths—but we don't follow through with our actions.

There is usually some personal cost for keeping our commitments to people. It may cost us time or money. Are we willing to pay the price? Are we willing to be a living example of Jesus? He never promised anything that He didn't do—no matter how much it cost Him. He willingly went to the cross to fulfill the promise God made back in Genesis that He would send a Savior. Talk about long-term commitment. And He hasn't quit on us yet.

Are you the light of the world in faithfulness, as God is?

One of the biggest tests of my faithfulness to God came through a Christian music company. I had fulfilled my two contracts with my record company and it was time to renegotiate.

Another larger Christian label started pursuing me with an incredible offer. They would set up a fund and put $100,000 in it for each record I agreed to do with them. The cost of each album would come out of that fund and whatever was left over from the $100,000 per album budget I got to keep. So if one album cost me $40,000, I could put the remaining

$60,000 into my own pocket as a personal bonus. They said they would do up to five albums with me using this arrangement.

It was tempting. I had so many visions and goals for Last Days Ministries that could have been accomplished with that amount of money.

But something about it didn't feel right. I wrestled with it. The money was great. And I was going to make the albums, no matter which company I signed with. But no matter how I looked at it, I couldn't find peace. Somehow I felt the devil was trying to buy me off—and my ministry wasn't for sale. I wanted to be faithful to the Lord. I didn't want to be seduced by all that money. So I turned and ran the other way.

The world needs to see a huge sunburst of faithfulness from Christians. Faithfulness in our marriages. Faithfulness in our financial dealings. Faithfulness in keeping our word. Jesus told a parable about gold talents, and He ended it this way: The master said to the servant, "Well done, good and faithful slave; you were faithful with a few things, I will put you in charge of many things; enter into the joy of your master" (Matthew 25:23).

Right now Jesus is watching us—His disciples—to see if we are fit for bigger responsibilities. And not only is He watching us, the world is watching us too. The question is, are we going to be accurate reflections of our Father's faithfulness?

Another thing the world needs to see in Christians is *integrity*. Jesus

---

If doing a good act in public will excite others to do more good, then . . . "Let your Light shine to all . . . " Miss no opportunity to do good.
—John Wesley

---

had integrity. He lived a life that was open for all to see. He wanted His disciples to see Him in every situation—in stress, in times of relaxation, in public and in private. Jesus was not like most of us today. We want people to see us in some situations, but not in others. We invite people to be with us when we're in public, but our private lives can be different. Jesus' enemies paid Him a backhanded compliment. The Pharisees tried to trap Him by sending some of their disciples to Jesus to say, "Teacher, we know that You are truthful and teach the way of God in truth, and defer to no one; for you are not partial to any" (Matthew 22:16). The guys who were most against Jesus acknowledged that He was a man who walked in truth. That means He acted the same way to all people in all circumstances. There was no hidden side to Jesus' personality—no "dark side" that He needed to hide. That's integrity.

People today are desperate to see in their lives that same integrity Jesus displayed.

David asked God to judge him:

> The Lord judges the peoples; vindicate me, O Lord,
> according to my righteousness and my integrity that is in
> me (Psalm 7:8).

Do we dare ask God to do the same with us? Is there integrity in our hearts?

The word *integrity* comes from the same root word as *integrate*. Integrity means to make the parts of something work together in a complete and cohesive whole. That's what God wants to do in our lives. He wants to break down the barriers we put up between the various parts of our life. He wants the way we treat our husband or wife and our kids to be integrated with the way we pray at prayer meetings. He wants the way we divide up our income to be integrated with what we teach others about giving. He wants the way we speak to others to be as pleasing to Him as the way we read the Bible out loud at church.

Do you turn your witness on and off like a faucet? Jesus opened all of His life for others to see. What would people see if you did the same? The Bible has a lot to say about being integrated people—people who allow the truth to invade not just a few areas, but every area of their lives.

We want to pick and choose which areas God works His nature into. That's how we know we need repentance. Before we become Christians we have areas of strength—special talents and abilities. But we also have areas of weakness, things we tend to ignore or tuck away out of sight. After our conversion, the Holy Spirit begins to work. His aim is wholeness. He wants to bring us to a place where all areas of our life are integrated and functioning for His glory.

Isaiah promised that when the Messiah came, "Every mountain and hill [shall] be made low; and let the rough ground become a plain" (Isaiah 40:4). This of course didn't happen in a literal sense—the mountains didn't cave in when Jesus was born. But in a personal sense, this change happens to people who follow Him in spirit. God wants to smooth out the rough edges in our lives. He wants to take the tops off the "mountains" and use them to fill in the "valleys," until we're balanced people of integrity. He wants our strengths to come under His authority, and He wants us to give Him our weaknesses—to let Him fill them in.

When I became a Christian there were many weak areas in my life that I was happy to ignore. But Jesus wanted to bring everything out into the open. He started to show me—and everybody around me—the weakest areas in my character. This was painful at first, but then I began to catch on. I saw that what He was doing was for my own good. A chain is only as strong as its weakest link, and my life was only as useful to God as my most *unsurrendered* and *unholy* area. So He wanted to make the weak areas of my life as strong as my strongest areas. And He wanted me to submit all of it to Him.

The Pharisees had tremendous strengths. Every day of a Pharisee's life was dominated by the Law of God. Every action was scrutinized by Old Testament Law. But balanced against this was their greatest weakness—their hard, legalistic hearts—hearts that would sooner bind others up than free them.

This is a warning: don't be like the Pharisees. Don't plow ahead only in your strong areas. Instead, ask the Lord to fill in the valleys in your life. Otherwise, you're headed for self-righteousness.

Do you want to be a person who's known for integrity? Someone whose actions match their words? Someone who's not hiding their weaknesses, but exposing them to the light of God's truth?

If our faith isn't integrated into our lives, then we're hypocrites. And our hypocrisy will be an unpleasant smell to everyone around us—and to God.

Here's another big issue—God wants to let His light shine through us as we love others.

Love! Oh we *do* like to use that word. Sounds so sweet, right?

The disciples saw Jesus with every conceivable type of person—even with the lowest of the low. They saw Him rescue the woman caught in adultery. There was never any argument over whether she was guilty, and under the law she deserved to be stoned. But she was released when Jesus challenged her persecutors about their own righteousness. There was no place in their law to reconcile anyone to God. It was all *law*, no *love*.

The disciples also saw Jesus talking to a Samaritan woman. It was unusual enough to see a man speaking meaningfully to a woman—but this woman was a sworn enemy of the Jewish people. According to their customs, Jesus shouldn't have had anything to do with her. But as she shared her water with Him, He pointed her towards salvation. The disciples wouldn't have touched the cup of water at all, because in their eyes it was *unclean*.

The list could go on and on. There was no social group that Jesus avoided. He healed the lepers and dined with the Pharisees. No one was rejected by Him because of their age or religion. No one was too educated or too ignorant for Jesus to care about.

How often do we look at superficial things and judge a person—without getting close enough to them to know what God's doing in their heart?

The disciples also saw Jesus deal with every conceivable *reaction* from people. But no behavior, no matter how bad, drove Him away.

People tried to trick Jesus. They challenged Him on theological matters. They were ready to kill Him. Some welcomed Him as an earthly king; others were ready to fight against Him. But Jesus was the same with all of them.

Think about how out of step Jesus was with the society around Him—and how radical His actions were. Jesus cut through all the labels we put on each other, and spoke directly to the hearts of men and women. And He challenged His disciples to do the same.

But so often we want to choose the social group, the age group or the religious group we would *prefer* to share the gospel with. What an attitude. Our life is a reflection of Jesus to everyone we meet, not just those we select. We can't say, "Jesus, I'll witness to my friend Pete—but I'm not interested in Fred. He's a real jerk." The Bible says, "While we were yet sinners Christ died for us." When we choose to leave out some sinners because we think they're too hard for the gospel, we're showing our ignorance of God's power—and we fail Him as disciples.

Jesus made it clear in the Sermon on the Mount:

"I say to you, love your enemies, and pray for those who persecute you in order that you may be sons of your Father who is in heaven; for He causes His sun to rise on the evil and the good, and sends rain on the righteous and the unrighteous. For if you love those who love you, what reward have you? Do not even the tax-gatherers do the same? And if you greet your brothers only, what do you do more than others? Do not even the Gentiles do the same? Therefore you are to be perfect, as your heavenly Father is perfect" (Matthew 5:44-48).

It's time for us to stop calling the shots about who we will go to and who we won't. Are we the hands and feet and face of Jesus to the world or not?

When you turn on a light it shines all over the place. It doesn't say, "I'll shine three feet to the left and six inches to the right." Are you the light of the world—or are you a hidden light?

You decide.

I want God to polish me until others look into my face and see the face of Jesus reflected back. I want them to see a face of acceptance and love. That's what it's going to take to call other people out of the darkness.

Jesus said,

"Why are

you sleeping?
Rise and pray…"

Luke 22:46

Pray
As A Servant

"Thy will be done, on earth as it is in heaven" (Matthew 6:10).

———————◆———————

Some Christians think of prayer only as a way to get what they need from God. They ask—He gives. Other people think of prayer as a time to worship Him. Or to quote His promises—to stand in faith for what they need. Or they think of it as a time to command powers and principalities to be gone in the name of Jesus. Or to sit God down and remind Him of their list of petitions. Prayer *can* be some of the above, but have you ever thought of prayer this way—as the time when God wants to reveal your own heart to you?

For instance, do you pray *always*—or only when you're in trouble or you need something? Do you whine and complain about people of God—is that what you think prayer is?

Think about being alone and having one of those hidden surveillance cameras trained on you—what would your prayer time look like if you had to watch it played back to you? Would you be yawning and glancing at the clock to see how soon you could get out of there? Would you be arguing with God? Or letting Him know how angry and disappointed you are that He didn't answer your requests the way you asked Him to?

If you take an honest, hard look at your prayer life, God will use it to sift through your heart. He will show you attitudes you have that are not the attitudes of a true servant of God—the attitudes of one who really knows his Master. You see, when our hearts are pure, we hear His voice—we pray wholeheartedly, and we obey wholeheartedly. What a combination. That's dynamite!

What are some of those wrong heart attitudes? What does God want to replace them with?

We need to ask ourselves, Do we really believe there is power in prayer—that prayer is effective? Or do we secretly think it's a waste of time?

"Praying" Hyde was a man who was convinced that prayer was powerful. He would go to a town, rent a hotel room, lock himself in and pray for people. Whole towns would experience revival as a result of his prayer. He didn't even have to preach. He just locked himself away and prayed and people came under conviction of sin. Do you know what Praying Hyde would do if he prayed for someone for two weeks and their life didn't change? He'd bury his head in the pillow and say, "Oh God, what have I done? Show me what sin has crept into my life that hinders you from answering." He knew that unanswered prayer wasn't God's fault. He knew that God is powerful, and that He always answers prayers. So when an answer was held up, Hyde searched his own heart to find the problem.

Praying Hyde was a man who took the words of Jesus literally when He said:

> "Therefore I say to you, all things for which you pray and ask, believe that you have received them, *and they shall be granted you*" (Mark 11:24, emphasis added).

The early church also took Jesus' words literally. Think of the great stories in Acts when prayers were answered in mighty ways. There was Peter's supernatural release from prison:

> Peter was kept in the prison, but prayer for him was being made fervently by the church to God...And behold, an angel of the Lord suddenly appeared, and a light shone in the cell; and he struck Peter's side and roused him, saying, "Get up quickly." And his chains fell off his hands (Acts 12:5, 7).

Think of the story of how a little girl was raised from the dead.

> Peter sent them all out and knelt down and prayed, and turning to the body, he said, "Tabitha, arise." And she opened her eyes, and when she saw Peter, she sat up. And he gave her his

hand and raised her up; and calling the saints and widows, he presented her alive. And it became known all over Joppa, and many believed in the Lord (Acts 9:40-42).

What is your heart-attitude about prayer? Some Christians are like the Buddhists with their prayer wheels. We give our "wheel" a few whirls a day, to make us feel pious. We pray so we won't feel guilty—guilt takes all the fun out of life. So we go through the motions. We spin our "wheels," hoping that we've done our duty. Yet, we really don't expect anything to happen.

This is so far from the truth about prayer. Prayer is not a duty—it is our lifeline. Prayer is the gas in our gas tank. It's the fuel that keeps our spiritual lives going. It's talking to God, listening to Him and then doing what He tells us to do. Prayer is close, intimate communion with the Lord. And it's the testimony of the early church. They knew they were God's friends and servants on earth. And they knew they needed to keep their hearts soft through prayer, so they'd stay alive spiritually.

Throughout the Bible, unanswered prayer is always a red flag—a signal that something is wrong. Scripture is clear as to why God sometimes does *not* answer the prayers of His people. If our prayers are not answered—if prayer is a routine we go through—then we need to examine our hearts. There may be a major spiritual block there—and getting rid of it is the key to getting our spiritual life back on track. We can continue on in our self-made worlds where mere guilt-relieving prayer is enough. Or we can ask the Holy Spirit to examine our hearts regarding each of these points. Then with a clear heart we can ask Him to teach us how to pray effective prayers—prayers that God hears and answers.

One reason we may think prayer is powerless, a waste of time, is that *we pray and nothing happens*. Then we decide it's God's fault. But maybe the Holy Spirit wants to show us something about our motives. Maybe they're *selfish*. James said,

> You ask and do not receive, because you ask with wrong motives, so that you may spend it on your pleasures (James 4:3).

James was very plain. We pray for a lot of things that are right to ask for, and that God might even be happy to give us. But the prayer falls powerless because its motive is selfish. Selfishness robs prayer of all power—mark that down. To pray with pure motives, we have to remember the true purpose of prayer—that *God* will be glorified in the answer.

Let's say that a woman is praying for her husband to be converted. That's a good thing to ask of God, right? But how often is a request like this tainted with subtle, selfish, impure motives. Sometimes a person wants their spouse to become a Christian so they'll stop drinking, smoking and swearing and become easier to live with. Or maybe they want someone they can be proud of, because their spouse embarrasses them. In their heart they've judged and despised the spouse—and God wants to reveal their hatefulness and pride. If we ask something of God out of selfish desire—even if it's deeply buried—James says God will not answer our prayer.

What should someone's motive be in asking for their spouse's salvation? First, that God will be glorified. We know we're praying in purity when we can't bear the thought of God, our heavenly Father, being dishonored by our unsaved husband or wife. When we can't stand to see the grace of God trampled underfoot, then our motive is not selfish.

Praying for revival is another thing that pleases God. But it's even possible to pray for revival with a selfish motive. Let's say you want revival to increase your church's membership. Or you want to make your ministry look good. Or you hope to give a good report at your denomination's annual conference. All of these reasons are polluted with selfish motives.

When does our revival praying become pure? When we cannot stand for God to be dishonored by the worldliness of the church. And because we sense God's broken heart over the sin of unbelievers. But if our minds are set on personal or corporate gain, our prayers are useless. God loves us too much to indulge us. He will not pander to our selfish needs and desires.

So, sometimes our deeper heart motives need to be exposed. Like Praying Hyde, we can open ourselves up to God, and He'll show us what's blocking the way.

Then again, many of us have another problem that's crushing the life out of our prayers: sin that we know about, but won't confess or forsake. Isaiah said,

> Behold, the Lord's hand is not so short that it cannot save;
> neither is His ear so dull that it cannot hear. But your iniquities have made a separation between you and your God, and

your sins have hidden His face from you, so that He does not hear (Isaiah 59:1-2).

God wasn't answering the Israelites' prayers anymore, so they came up with some interesting theories as to why not. Some decided that God was getting a little old, that His hands were shriveling up. Maybe He was

———————◆———————

Get alone with Jesus and either tell Him that you do not want sin to die out in you—or else tell Him that at all costs you want to be identified with His death.

— Oswald Chambers

———————◆———————

getting arthritis, and didn't have the strength. Possibly He was going deaf. How could they trust a tired old grandfather in the sky? What other reason could there be for their unanswered prayers?

Isaiah shook his head. "You've thought of everything except the obvious," he said. "God hasn't changed. You have. Your sins are cutting off your communication with Him. God can't hear what you're saying because of your sin."

People cry out to God in vain, because there is known sin in their lives. Sin from their past that's unconfessed, or some sin they're secretly indulging in now. They forget the words of David:

> If I regard wickedness in my heart, the Lord will not hear (Psalm 66:18).

If we want powerful, effective prayer, then we have to be ruthless about our sin. We have to let God put His finger on the things in our lives that displease Him. We should pray like this:

> Search me, O God, and know my heart: try me, and know my thoughts: and see if there be any wicked way in me (Psalm 139:23-24, KJV).

Believe it—God *will* reveal our sins. We should confess, repent and be done with them.

I remember praying one time for two definite things. Both of these things needed to happen or God would be dishonored. I prayed and prayed, but the answer never came. The night before the prayer absolutely had to be answered, I woke up in the dark. I cried out to God to answer my prayer. I reasoned with Him about how I needed Him to act. Still no answer.

I pleaded. I begged. Finally, out of desperation, I asked God to show me if there was anything wrong in my life. Immediately, God brought something to mind. It was sin He'd brought to my attention before, but I'd been unwilling to confess it as sin. I justified it. When we justify sin we're stuck with it.

That night I said to God, "If that's what's wrong, then I'll give it up." A pretty good prayer. But still no answer came. "God," I said again, "If that's sin, then I repent." *Still no answer.*

Finally, I came out with it: "God, I acknowledge that as sin. I repent of it. I give it up." I found peace. In a few minutes I was sleeping like a baby.

In the morning the answer to my prayer came, and God's name was honored.

Once we confess and repent of any sin in our life, then we *will* experience a new power in our prayer. God can then answer our prayers. We won't need to look for creative excuses for why He didn't answer. God delights to answer the prayers of those whose hearts are clean before Him.

Another reason our prayer lives go dead is that we sometimes refuse to be honest with God. It's not just sinful actions we hide. We pretend we're full of joy and love when we're not. But God knows.

> Thou dost scrutinize my path and my lying down, and art intimately acquainted with all my ways. Even before there is a word on my tongue, behold, O Lord, Thou dost know it all (Psalm 139:3-4).

Prayer isn't some kind of show. We can't fool God into thinking everything is rosy when we're really depressed and hurting. Or when we're full of thoughts of revenge toward someone, and we want to pretend everything's just wonderful. We have to be real with God. We need to admit exactly how we're feeling.

The Psalms are probably the most honest prayers ever recorded. They're full of gritty reality. David takes us through the full range of human emotions. He is real with God. As a result, he experienced God's power in his life.

There are times when I felt I was praying to brass walls. Not so long ago it felt like that. I got down on my knees. I didn't try to work up my emotions. I didn't say, "Oh, Jesus, I'm going to worship you. I'm going to praise you." I didn't try to fool God. He knew what I was feeling. I just knelt there and said, "God, I can't pray. I come to you—not on my own merit, but in the name of Jesus. I don't even feel like praying." And God whispered into my heart, "Okay, be quiet." So I was quiet. Then, bam! My emotions began to well up, and I had a wonderful, peaceful time of fellowship with the Lord. Such a powerful time would never have been possible if I'd spent the time trying to fake it with God.

Be honest with God about how you feel. You can't hide it. He knows before you ever admit it, and He wants you to trust Him with how you feel. He wants you to be real with Him.

When we admit our frailty to God and rely upon Him, He releases His strength and power to us. That power shows itself in our prayer times.

Then of course there's this thing called *obedience*. A lot of our prayers fall to the ground because we have not done what He has already told us to do.

> Has the Lord as much delight in burnt offerings and sacrifices as in obeying the voice of the Lord? Behold, to obey is better than sacrifice, and to heed than the fat of rams (1 Samuel 15:22).

That's an interesting verse. God doesn't care how eloquent our prayer is. He doesn't care how earnest we are when we pray. He doesn't care where we pray. What He cares about is whether we did the last thing He told us to do. God wants our obedience.

Perhaps God impressed you to do something as simple as making restitution to a person you have wronged. Sometimes we say to God,

"Oh, sure. But give me a couple of days to pray about it." Think how God must look at our response. It's like one of my kids coming up to me and saying, "What do you want me to do today?" It's a great question. All parents dream of their children asking that question. Suppose I say, "Go out and wash the car." My kid looks me right in the eye and says, "Well, let me go ask my dad." And I say, "Hey, wake up! Here I am. I just told you to go wash the car."

For the first few years of my music ministry I was really uncertain about how to handle the money part. To me my music is a tool to share Jesus. I'm not an entertainer, I'm a minister. I wasn't in it for the money, but it did pay our bills. We had lots of people living with us in several houses—which meant lots of food and big light bills.

Christian musicians handle money in many different ways. Some sell tickets to their concerts, some don't go anywhere unless they are guaranteed a certain amount up front, and a few go for love offerings.

How much do you charge a church to come and minister? Is it right to even charge anything? These questions kept me up at night because I wanted to hear God. And the Lord spoke clearly to me. I was to give free concerts and take love offerings. If I was in a setting, like a festival, where an offering couldn't be taken—then I could receive an honorarium. The Lord spoke similarly to Buck and Annie Herring, formerly with the singing group, The Second Chapter of Acts.

The people who came to the concerts were blessed, but some people in the Christian music industry got upset. One agent who booked other Christian artists was almost angry. My concerts and those of The Second Chapter of Acts were some of the biggest Christian concerts in America at the time, and the agent said to me, "If the high-profile artists do concerts for free it makes everybody else look bad." But that wasn't what I was trying to do. I was just trying to be obedient to the Lord.

I knew I had to do what God wanted me to do. I couldn't go back and say, "Well, God, I didn't obey your first order—but give me another one and I'll do better."

You don't *pray about* something God plainly *tells* you to do. You do it. What you're saying to God when you keep on praying about something He's told you to do is, "This isn't really what I had in mind. I'll just put it on hold and see if You tell me what I want to hear." Often we're unprepared for the mundane things God asks us to do. We want to hear Him tell us to do spectacular things. Glamorous things. Things that bring *us* glory, not God.

If we've hamstrung our relationship with God through disobedience, then our prayers will not be answered. When God hears our prayers He'll say, "That's such a fervent prayer. If only you would obey my voice with the same fervency, then I could *really* answer that prayer." Doing all that God has told you to do—that's vital to having your prayers answered.

A little while ago we were talking about sin. I want to talk now about something that's just as serious—or worse: idolatry. Putting something else in the place of God. God told Ezekiel,

> "Son of man, these men have set up their idols in their hearts, and have put right before their faces the stumbling block of their iniquity. Should I be consulted by them at all?" (Ezekiel 14:3).

God is saying, "Why should I even listen to these people? They have idols in their hearts."

Do you have an idol in your life? A wrong relationship? A career? A possession? Having an idol is a major block in our relationship with God, and it will kill our prayers.

You don't have to have a little god set up in your living room, or make sacrifices on a pagan altar in your bedroom to have an idol in your life. An idol is anything that takes the place of God in your heart. Anything that becomes the object of your devotion. My singing can become idolatry when I'm singing to sing, not singing to Jesus. Prayer can become idolatry when I'm only asking for items on my prayer list and not praying to God. Bible reading can become idolatry if I'm doing it simply to get theological information, and not to know God better. In fact, there are people studying for the ministry in seminaries all over the country who don't know Jesus. The Bible is their idol, their God. They worship knowledge of God, rather than God himself. God alone has the right to the supreme place in our hearts.

Religious practices can be an idol. Or a new house or car. Even your husband or wife or kids. If something takes God's place in your life, it's an idol.

If your prayers are not answered then ask yourself, "Is God first in my life?" If not, it's impossible for us to prevail in prayer. God will *not* be second-best in our lives.

There's one big idol that wants to take over our hearts—*money*. Talk about something that really sifts the heart.

You know, God wants us to be joyful, happy givers. Liberal givers. And there's a warning we need to heed:

> He who shuts his ear to the cry of the poor will also cry himself and not be answered (Proverbs 21:13).

Do you realize that stinginess hinders prayer? If you don't respond to cries for help from God's children, then God won't respond to your cries. Sounds legalistic, but it's not. It's just that how you handle money reveals your heart. If God has your money, He knows He's got your heart. But He also wants us to be liberal in offering forgiveness. Liberal with lending and giving our material possessions. Liberal with our time. Liberal in sharing our skills. It's not surprising that the prayers of many churches are not answered. Too often, they're only concerned with themselves—about the color of the new pew cushions, about the loan to build a new building, about increasing the pastor's salary, and *not* about pouring out their time, talent and money to meet the needs of the poor and needy.

Listen to this statement about prevailing prayer, in 1 John:

> Whatever we ask we receive from Him, because we keep His commandments and do the things that are pleasing in His sight (1 John 3:22).

What pleases God? According to Proverbs 21:13, it's listening to the poor when they cry for help, and responding to them. God responds to those who give to the poor. He answers their prayers, and pours out His blessing. So, the generous man can be a mighty man of prayer. The stingy man becomes powerless in prayer.

Maybe you see that most of the negative heart-attitudes have a positive flip side. Our prayers *will* be answered when we pray with a pure heart, and we pray according to God's will. John says,

> And this is the confidence which we have before Him, that, if we ask anything according to His will, He hears us (1 John 5:14).

The way to prevail in prayer is to work *with* God. We need to talk *and* to listen in order to know His will. And when we know His will, we can pray *according* to His will—and He promises to hear us and answer. It's that simple. That's our confidence.

Despite being that simple, many of us still seem to miss it. We're busy asking for things that are not His will. Selfish, self-indulgent things. Things that will bring glory to us and not to God. Or things that don't have the best interests of others at heart. Some of these things may not be bad—they're just outside the will of God. We pray, "If only you'd help pay my bills, Lord, then I'd do your will." God says, "Do my will. Do you know what it is?"

God looks for people to whom He can reveal the desires of His heart. People who will do His will joyfully. God hears and answers the prayers of these people, and He takes care of them. Are you one of these people, or do you only delight in doing *your* will? Did you know that God's will for your life is the only thing that will bring you fulfillment and joy? He has great things in store for you—if you'll only take off the blinders of self-seeking long enough. If you'll just give Him one minute to show you His will—for your life and for the world around you, all the Christians in need, all the people going to hell....

That brings me to my last point. God answers prayer when our hearts are desperate for Him. James says,

> You do not have because you do not ask (James 4:2).

This word that's translated *ask* in our Bibles really means "to crave." James was saying, "You don't have, because you don't *crave it from me.*"

The people of Israel got into some desperate situations in the wilderness, and God met their needs in miraculous ways. When they were so thirsty they couldn't go on, God met their need. The only water they found to drink was contaminated. There was no 7-Eleven where they could buy a Coke to quench their thirst. So Moses *cried out* to the Lord, and the Lord showed him a tree. He cut the tree down and threw it into the contaminated water. The water was purified and all Israel was able to drink (Exodus 15:22-27).

That's the kind of desperation God wants from us. He wants us to come to the point where we're so thirsty for Him to answer that we can't go on without hearing His voice. When He sees that kind of desperation, when He sees that we're totally dependent upon Him, when He sees that He is our only hope—then He answers every time.

When was the last time you were that desperate in your prayers?

Too many of us are still back at that place where we're blaming God for not answering our prayers. In our hearts, we think He's indifferent—or that He's a weak, old grandpa.

Charles Finney once visited a church where the congregation had prayed for years for a revival in their town. As Finney listened to their prayers he was horrified. Every elder in the church stood and prayed like this: "Oh God, we have prayed now for many years and you have not answered. Lord why aren't You answering our prayers? Why can't You hear us? Why have You not answered?"

Finally, they invited Finney to speak, and he said he got up with an "explosion" in his heart. "Do I take it that you're blaming God for not answering your prayers?" he asked. Then he began to preach about repentance from selfishness and sin. At first, the congregation stared at him with cold and angry looks.

Then one of the elders burst into tears, fell on his knees and called out, "Brother Finney, it's all true!" Then the rest of the congregation did the same, and revival broke out.

For the first time, these people stopped blaming God for not answering their prayers and saw where the problem was all along—in their hard hearts.

There is no magic formula for effective prayer. The only important thing is our heart attitude.

Is your heart soft with love for God? Do you want to see glory and honor brought to His name from the answer to your prayer? Are you willing to obey His will and do what He tells you to do?

Prayers *should* be answered. If yours haven't been, check your heart.

If you're not receiving answers to your prayers, it's probably not that God is saying, "Wait." More likely it's that God is trying to get your attention. Trying to point out an area in your life where your heart attitude is wrong. Don't let a molehill in your heart grow into a mountain that blocks your effectiveness in prayer. Ask God to reveal your heart to you. Correct the areas that need correction. And be fervent in prayer, expecting God to answer.

Never settle for a powerless Christian life. We are called to be servants of God. And God wants us to prevail, with prayers that bring the rule of His kingdom to this world.

Jesus said,

"…Love your enemies…

   give to the needy…

 pray in secret…

  fast…

do not store up treasures on earth…

   seek first [God's] kingdom

  and His righteousness…"

      Matthew 5, 6

Have Faith That Conquers Worldliness

What use is it, my brethren, if a man says he has faith, but he has no works? Can that faith save him? If a brother or sister is without clothing and in need of daily food, and one of you says to them, "Go in peace, be warmed and be filled," and yet you do not give them what is necessary for their body, what use is that? Even so faith, if it has no works, is dead, being by itself. But someone may well say, "You have faith, and I have works; show me your faith without the works, and I will show you my faith by my works" (James 2:14-18).

James challenges all of us who call ourselves Christians: "You say you have faith. Where is it? Show it to me." It's a good question, a disturbing question: How do we show our faith in Jesus Christ?

Faith is not something you can pull out of a drawer and spread out on a little velvet mat for people to admire. "Oh, look at Sue's faith. Isn't it great? It's much better than Danny's faith." You can't isolate faith like that.

James' challenge should stop us in our tracks. He says we can't get by with some of the pat things we say. "Faith? Oh sure! I believe in my heart, and I don't think other people need to know about my faith. It's a private matter between me and God." That's not the attitude of a disciple. What that attitude really says is "I know I'm going to heaven, and that's all I was really after."

Faith is a *gift of God,* and He wants us to let it be seen. Faith is supposed to be worked out in our lives so everyone can see it and give glory to our Father in heaven.

Our faith should motivate us to reach out to others and tell them the good news. To give them food. To visit them in prison. To open our homes to them, if necessary. We can't say we'll do the faith part and let someone who has a "ministry of giving" do the rest. Each of us shows our faith by the things we do with the money, time and talents God has given us.

I guess people in James' day were like us—they thought there was a class of *super-Christians* who had faith, and others who just naturally had a servant's heart. James said, "No way! Without works your faith is dead. Fit to be buried. If faith doesn't produce a change in the way we live, it's worthless." Our faith is the yeast that changes the way we live. Faith isn't the printed-out recipe—it's the active ingredient.

Now sometimes we confuse the works James talks about with dead works. Doing things to prove to God we're good enough for Him to save us.

It's not enough to go around giving out tracts to the hungry, the dying, the homeless and the helpless—to smile at them and say, "Jesus loves you." We offer salvation to people, but never stop long enough to look at them with compassion as Jesus did. We forget to feed them so that their stomachs will stop gnawing long enough for them to hear the gospel. And we don't see that as hypocritical. How can we see their spiritual need but overlook their physical need?

William Booth, founder of the Salvation Army, said that no one who had a toothache could really pay attention to the gospel. Do we get the point? We've got to take care of a person's physical pain as we minister to the spiritual pain in their heart.

That takes a deeper commitment, doesn't it?

We're not on this earth just to tell others the good news. We're here to *live out* the good news for everyone to see. Paul tells us,

> We are His workmanship, created in Christ Jesus for good works, which God prepared beforehand, that we should walk in them (Ephesians 2:10).

Are we really interested in the good works that Christ has planned for us to do? Are we open to a faith that is living and active—that changes us into willing servants? To be willing means to become His bondservants, so that everything we are and all that we have is at God's disposal. Not that we run out and give all our possessions to the poor just to prove we're radical Christians. That's a dead work, if we're trying to prove something to God. But if we refuse to see that all we own belongs to the Lord, then we're playing games with Him. God has only made us *stewards* over things. God gives us our bodies, our time and our possessions so that we can use them to bless and minister to other people.

Once the Lord told me to drive a guy from Hollywood, California all the way to Tucson, Arizona. He was a genuinely nice guy—but he didn't know the Lord. We'd met through a mutual friend, and when I found out he was catching the bus to Tucson the next day, I heard the Lord say to me, "You take him." He thought I was crazy when I told him—and so did my friends. But he was "ripe" for Jesus. I preached to him all the way to Tucson, and along the way he gave his heart to the Lord. He's still serving the Lord today.

It was an out-of-the-ordinary thing to do. But my obedience to the Lord and giving of my time brought another soul into the kingdom of God.

That's what we're talking about. Showing our faith to others in practical ways so they'll be blessed by it.

Jesus made this very plain. He used a great parable to illustrate it.

> "Now there was a certain rich man, and he habitually dressed in purple and fine linen, gaily living in splendor every day. And a certain poor man named Lazarus was laid at his gate, covered with sores, and longing to be fed...Now it came about that the poor man died and he was carried away...and the rich man also died and was buried. And in Hades he...saw Abraham far away, and Lazarus in his bosom. And he cried out and said, 'Father Abraham, have mercy on me...for I am in agony in this flame.' But Abraham said, 'Child, remember that during your life you received your good things, and likewise Lazarus bad things; but now he is being comforted here, and you are in agony" (Luke 16:19-25).

Sometimes I deceive myself into thinking I'm better than the rich man. I think, "If someone was left outside my door, of course I'd take care of his needs." Then how is it that people are starving a few thousand miles away from where I live, and I think I can ignore them?

Do we think that because a famine or a disaster happens in some part of the world where we don't see it everyday that we're not responsible to help? Does God care that they are thousands of miles away, starving, while we go on living in abundance? To God there is no distance. The ends of the universe are His walls. Since we are His children, what happens within His four walls should concern us, too. The Father has chosen us to be His hands and His feet to minister to people *anywhere we know there is need and hurt.*

What's the limit of your concern? In the evening we love to sit in our air-conditioned living rooms and watch TV. There on the news we see faces of dying, starving, helpless people. We see people afflicted by war, famine, disease and other natural disasters. These people aren't being laid at our gate—they're being laid in our living rooms. They look us straight in the eye as we kick back in our cushioned recliners. "Could you bring me some more gravy, dear? My goodness, look at these starving people! Would you mind changing the channel? This is upsetting my dinner."

Are we going to leave the homeless and starving lying helplessly on our living room rug?

Or, we get our mail, and the first thing we do is sort out the "junk" and toss it in the garbage. You know what we count as junk?—the pleas for help from relief agencies. The request for funds for an unwed mother's home. The missionary needing support. These are needs that are laid at our gate, and we throw them in the trash can.

You can say, "Well, there's a limit to what I can give." Okay—what's the limit? Who set it?

God will require us to account for every need we turn away, if we are too selfish to care. Jesus said the person who has two coats should give one to the person who has none (Luke 3:11). Maybe you don't personally know someone who has no coat. But we all know that there are children in our inner-cities, in Mexico and Asia, who don't have coats. In today's media-oriented world, there's not a person who can say, "Hey, I didn't realize there are people out there who are cold." If we didn't know about these needs, we'd have an excuse. But as Jesus said to the Pharisees,

> "If you were blind, you would have no sin; but since you say, 'We see,' your sin remains" (John 9:41).

This brings us back to James. He put it this way:

> Therefore, to one who knows the right thing to do, and does not do it, to him it is sin (James 4:17).

Jesus *commanded* us to reach out to the poor and the needy. We know who those people are. The question is, what are we doing for them?

It's not easy ministering to people's needs, because it's not the natural thing to do. Our flesh tries to think of ways to get out of it. We have endless justifications and excuses for not doing what God has told us to do. Listen to this:

> A certain lawyer stood up and put [Jesus] to the test, saying, "Teacher, what shall I do to inherit eternal life?" And [Jesus] said to him, "What is written in the Law? How does it read to you?" [The lawyer] answered and said, "You shall love the Lord your God with all your heart, and with all your soul, and with all your strength, and with all your mind; and your neighbor as yourself." And [Jesus] said to him, "You have answered correctly; do this and you will live." But wishing to justify himself, he said to Jesus, "And who is my neighbor?" (Luke 10:25-29).

Jesus knew this guy's heart—and He knows ours. So He told the story of the Good Samaritan. Most of us know it—how the priest and the Levite both hurried by on the other side of the road to avoid the man who'd been robbed. We know that it was a despised Samaritan who took pity on him.

After He told this story, Jesus asked the lawyer,

> "Which of these three do you think proved to be a neighbor to the man who fell into the robbers' hands?" And he said, "The one who showed mercy toward him." And Jesus said to him, "Go and do the same" (Luke 10:36-37).

Go—and help! It's a commandment that's repeated over and over in the Bible. John was pretty blunt when he told us our obligation:

We know love by this, that He laid down His life for us; and we ought to lay down our lives for the brethren. But whoever has the world's goods, and beholds his brother in need and closes his heart against him, how does the love of God abide in him? (1 John 3:16-17).

How can we say, "It's not my responsibility. I don't have a burden for this person. I don't feel led. It's not my ministry"? Can God really dwell in a heart that's closed to the needs of other people?

Don't fool yourself. When we begin to obey God, we will need to make radical changes in our lifestyles. Recently, God began to deal with me about this whole area of lifestyle. It really affected us. Melody and I used to eat out a lot. But God convicted us that we were not to eat out as often. If there was any way possible, we were to eat at home instead. So we began making meals at home for about a third of what it had cost us to buy them in a restaurant. Sure, it's nice to have somebody else cook and clean up and deliver a meal to your table. But we were convinced that it was a waste of God's money to pay somebody to do for us what we could easily do for ourselves. Now the money we save by eating at home we give to help the poor. It was such a little thing, but it came out of changed hearts.

Everyone can ask God to show them some way to do similar things. God is looking for people who will put themselves and their resources on the altar for His use. Not just our leftovers, but our first fruits.

Jesus rebuked the Pharisees for merely giving out of their excess. It was "easy" giving. He saw these very pious guys giving the equivalent of a thousand dollars to the temple treasury. Then a widow came along and put two cents in the collection. And Jesus said,

> "Truly, I say to you, this poor widow put in more than all the contributors to the treasury; for they all put in out of their surplus, but she, out of her poverty, put in all she owned, all she had to live on" (Mark 12:43-44).

It's easy to out-give a rich man. You only have to give from your heart. Jesus doesn't look at the *amount* we give, he looks at what it *costs us* to give it—what it costs us to give up something in order to minister to others.

Jesus is talking about *sacrifice.*

There are times when we no longer need something—for example, a coat—and we give it away, thinking we're obeying the Scripture. The person who receives it needs the coat, and says, "Praise God!" And we think we've given in generosity. But the truth is, we gave away something that we were ready to throw out. We gave it away to make room for the new leather or mink coat we really wanted. That's no sacrifice. That's not the kind of lifestyle Jesus wants us to live. He wants to use everything He has entrusted to us. Our generosity shows that our whole life is in His hands, and that our faith is not vain.

Many people are like the rich man in the story of Lazarus—too busy with their splendid living. Sure, they do "Christian" things, but they never focus their hearts on people who need help. They have no idea that it's possible to hallelujah, praise-the-Lord, and bumper-sticker your way to hell.

Our lives should be like Jesus Christ's, who constantly ministered to those in need. It's time we started living the life Jesus calls us to live.

Jesus never said it would be easy. I think it's part of the battle of faith. I struggle with knowing how many material things to own here on earth. But we can't decide on our own. We need God to guide us. Jesus said if we are His sheep we will hear His voice (John 10:27). He told the disciples that He would send a comforter who would lead them into all truth (John 14:16). That comforter was the Holy Spirit. Today we thrive on rules. Rules for this. Rules for that. We're so busy keeping the rules that sometimes we miss the Spirit's leading. Jesus never made up a set of rules for giving. Neither did Paul. God isn't interested in how many rules we can keep. He's interested in whether we hear His voice and obey it. And if we will listen to the leading of the Spirit, He'll show us how to relate to the material things we own.

The point is, Jesus wants us to follow Him with our whole heart. That means different things to different people at different times. For example, Jesus told the rich young ruler to sell all his possessions and give the money to the poor (Matthew 19:21). The New Testament doesn't record Jesus telling anyone else to do that.

In fact, think about the woman with the jar of expensive perfume. She poured it over Jesus' head, and the disciples were disgusted. They said, "What a waste." They thought about all the other things they could have done with the money it cost to buy that perfume. Jesus rebuked them and said, "...the poor you have with you always" (Matthew 26:11).

Was Jesus contradicting himself? Was He being inconsistent? No, He meant that we should never love the poor more than Him. "Love me *in* the poor," He was saying. "As you do this to the least of my brethren, you are doing it to me" (Matthew 25:40). We *have* been called to serve the poor. But we can only serve the poor when we recognize that we're really serving Jesus by doing so.

Living the lifestyle of a disciple of Jesus requires that we ask ourselves some basic questions: Are we willing to open up our homes and our wallets? Are we willing to allow needy people to come in and maybe dirty up our new carpet and our sofa? Are we willing to be inconvenienced for the sake of others? Will we let people come in and invade our privacy and our

---◆---

Believe steadfastly in what you have seen...Always go forward along the path of obedience...even if it seems to be leading you where you fear...

—Hannah Hurnard

---◆---

rights? Remember, as Christians, we're not meant to have rights.

There's another important question we need to ask: Are we willing to follow Jesus to the point of being ridiculed by others—even by our Christian friends? Unfortunately, other Christians often hold us back from doing the will of God.

I thought recently about how different things would be if I used the Bible as my only standard for living. I realized I'd be living a lot differently than I am now. And I thought about why. I came to the conclusion that what keeps me back is the way I serve the opinions of other Christians more than I serve God. The opinion of a person who is far away from God doesn't worry me. If an unbeliever says to me, "I don't like the way you said 'Praise the Lord,'" it wouldn't stop me from saying it. But if a Christian says, "Brother, I don't think that's the way the Lord would have us do it," I feel condemned. It's the response of other Christians—and my own sinful need for their approval—that can make me change the way I serve God.

We love to sing the hymn "I Have Decided to Follow Jesus"—especially the part that goes, "Though none go with me, still I will follow." But we don't practice it. Someone gets a bumper sticker, and pretty soon we've all got bumper stickers. If other Christians started riding to church on pogo sticks with little fish on them, we'd be doing it too. If someone tells us it's spiritually mature to pray a certain way, we'll do it that way. It is easy to be molded into each other's images, and hard to be molded to the image of Christ. We need to repent, because that shows that we want to please each other more than we want to please God. We need to get our eyes off others—even other Christians—and back on the Lord. We're on this earth to please Him, not other people—and that includes the way we use our possessions.

Why is this whole area of handling our possessions so important? Why does the Bible talk so much about it? Why does God care anyway? In some ways, money and possessions are the ultimate test of our faith. Jesus said:

> "No one can serve two masters; for either he will hate the one and love the other, or he will hold on to one and despise the other. You cannot serve God and mammon" (Matthew 6:24).

Have you let God be Master of your money and all that you own? Or are you mastered by these things? Does your money serve God—or does it control you?

We may think we're masters of our wealth—that we're using it to buy peace or pleasure. But we're blind and in a death trap. If we resist the Holy Spirit in order to hold onto our material possessions, we've been caught by the devil's bait. God will hold us accountable for our choice. Instead, we should obey God, give to relieve suffering here and store up treasure for ourselves in heaven. This kind of faith will radically change our whole life.

Someone recently told this story about a Christian who died and went to heaven. When he got there, God took him into a room and opened a huge cupboard full of emeralds, diamonds and every other precious stone you could imagine. The man said, "Wow! All these things are for me?" God shook his head. "No. That's all you *could* have had. It's the reward I wanted to give you when you got here."

If you listen to a lot of preachers today, you'd think that God wanted nothing more than to fill our pockets and our bank accounts.

Jesus *never* built up treasures on earth. He told us that we shouldn't either. He told us to lay up treasures in heaven (Matthew 6:20). How?

> He who is gracious to a poor man lends to the Lord, and He will repay him for his good deed (Proverbs 19:17).

This is the only place in the Bible where it says we can lend to the Lord. Not give, but lend. Lending implies we'll be paid back. The Lord keeps it on His account when we give. He says, "Put it on my bill. I will take care of it. You will get your investment back." He will reward us, as long as we don't seek the praise of others as our reward.

> "But when you give alms, do not let your left hand know what your right hand is doing that your alms may be in secret; and *your Father who sees you in secret will repay you*" (Matthew 6:3-4, emphasis added).

What kind of reward is waiting for us in heaven? That's a sobering question.

The Church has become polluted with compromise and hypocrisy. We've gotten far away from the Bible. But Jesus has a word for us:

> "And from everyone who has been given much shall much be required; and to whom they entrusted much, of him they will ask all the more" (Luke 12:48).

God is calling us back. It's time to put ourselves and all we own at God's disposal. He will not waste us—He'll *invest* us!

Yes, we're saved by grace and not by works. But our works prove that we are saved. An apple tree *becomes* an apple tree as a gift from God. But it *proves* it's an apple tree by producing apples.

It's time for us to lay aside our preoccupation with splendid living and open up our gates to see the poor and the needy people God has laid at our feet.

Jesus said,

"…your Father,

who sees

[what is done] in secret …

will repay you…

if therefore the light

that is in you is darkness,

how great is the darkness!"

Matthew 6:6, 23

11

Beware

Spiritual Coldness

But now that you have come to know God, or rather to be known by God, how is it that you turn back again to the weak and worthless elemental things, to which you desire to be enslaved all over again? (Galatians 4:9).

Have you taken a look at your life recently and thought, "Gee, where did God go? He was here a few days ago…or was it last week?" Have you felt cold toward God lately?

If your faith is going cold, it isn't God who cooled off. Spiritual coldness is a problem we have to watch out for—constantly.

There's a story I love to tell. It's about a woman who lives in a typical suburb, and who struggles with finding enough money to make ends meet. At two o'clock one afternoon, as she was looking over her checkbook balance, there was a knock at the door. She opened the door, and found a strange man there. He smiled, took a hundred-dollar bill out of his wallet and gave it to her. "There must be some mistake," she said. "I don't know you. This can't be for me."

"This is number 552, isn't it?" asked the man.

"Well, yes but…."

"Don't ask questions. Just accept the money. It's for you," the man insisted. Then he turned and walked away.

The woman stood in her doorway staring at the hundred-dollar bill. She was overcome with joy and gratitude. She called up all her friends and told them what had happened. She was so excited she couldn't sleep that night.

The next day—at the same time, there was another knock on her door. It was the same man holding another hundred-dollar bill.

"This is incredible! What's your name? Why are you doing this?" she asked.

"It's something I want to do for you" was all he said.

"Are you going to come back? Will I see you tomorrow?"

"Maybe," he replied.

This woman went out and bought the biggest thank-you card she could find. She baked cookies to have ready in case the man showed up again. Sure enough, the next afternoon at two o'clock the man was back with another hundred-dollar bill. She gave him the card and the cookies. Then she started baking more cookies for the next day. It was her way of showing gratitude.

Four days, five days, six days...on and on it went. Every afternoon at two o'clock the man was there with a hundred-dollar bill. This lady was thrilled. Every day she waited expectantly for the man to arrive.

After several months, though, she got tired of baking cookies. And besides that, having to be home every afternoon was a hassle. Getting the money was a blessing—but it took so much of her time. So she typed a letter to the man: "I'm sorry that I'm not at home to receive the hundred dollars. Please leave it in the envelope provided and slip it under the door. Thank you. P.S. I can't bake anymore. You appear to have plenty of money. So if you need cookies, there's a wonderful bakery on the next block."

For a few days this seemed to work—but one day there was no money in the envelope. The woman panicked. She needed the extra income. Her credit cards were maxed-out. She had new shoes on layaway. And what about the vacation home she was saving for?

The following day, she stayed home to see what had gone wrong. At two o'clock she peered through the window, and there was the same man—knocking on her *neighbor's* door!

"Wait!" she yelled as she ran out her front door. "You have the wrong house."

The man turned and gave her a puzzled look. "This is number 554, isn't it? It's your neighbor's turn. Why do you look so upset?"

We're all a bit like this woman. It's easy for us to live the Christian life when we're brand-new babes in Christ and the blessings are coming in like hundred-dollar bills. Then God seems to be constantly blessing us, constantly surprising us with His faithfulness and generosity. We say, "Wow! I don't deserve this. This is incredible—and God still has *more* for me? What can I do in return for you, God?"

So God says that He wants us to tell others about Him. And we say, "Sure, I'll go do that right now."

And then the Lord tells us He wants us to give our car to a brother in need. And we say, "No problem. Anything else I can do for you?"

But as we go on, we get used to the blessings flowing in every day. Our attitude changes. We begin to think, "But you gave me that—as a blessing. Surely you don't mean for *me* to give it away. I thought it was all for *me*."

It's easy to take God for granted. When we focus on the *gift* more than the Giver, we forget what it was like before we knew Jesus. Our enthusiasm begins to fade and we become dry and hard-hearted.

I've seen people give their hearts to the Lord thinking it would be smooth sailing from there. All they wanted was an easier life. They didn't want to belong to God, to honor Him and make Him happy. They were just looking for God to make them happy. And when He didn't, they quit.

One guy came to our home fellowship and prayed the "sinner's prayer." He was totally gung-ho...for about three weeks. He was out preaching on the streets and witnessing to all of his friends. But when he hit some opposition and all his friends didn't think he was so cool any-more, he decided this "Jesus stuff" wasn't for him.

The world is filled with people who have made a stab at being Christian. When Jesus doesn't pay up like they expected, they split, saying it didn't work for them.

In Revelation, Jesus judges the seven churches. The first one is the Ephesian church. He says:

> "I know your deeds and your toil and perseverance, and that you cannot endure evil men, and you put to the test those who call themselves apostles, and they are not, and you found them to be false; and you have perseverance and have endured for My name's sake, and have not grown weary" (Revelation 2:2-3).

Wait a minute—this sounds like a description of the perfect church.

How could things be any better? These people worked hard at the Christian life. They stayed away from evil. When so-called apostles came into their fellowship, they tested them to see if they were for real. And they had a hundred-percent success rate at spotting false apostles. Impressive. They'd suffered all sorts of problems and were ready to face more. These were mature Christians, right?

But read on—what's this? God wasn't happy with them.

> "But I have this against you, that you have left your first love" (Revelation 2:4).

"The truth," Jesus says, "is that something here has died and turned rotten. You don't have the sweet innocence, the love that you started out with. You're serving me out of habit and duty. You expect me to do all these things for you—but there's no heart left in our relationship." All the wonderful things these Ephesian Christians did right meant nothing in comparison to losing their first love for God.

When most of us came to the Lord, we knew we were totally helpless. After we received Him into our lives we wanted to spend as much time with Him as we could. We wanted to talk to Him about everything. We wanted to study the Bible, and we loved to fellowship with other Christians.

But three or four years later, we've learned our Bible. We've learned how to pray. We've learned how to sing and praise the Lord. We can speak fluent "Christianese." We know how to "feel led," how to "have a burden" and how to "put things on the altar." We know all the right words. All in all, we feel pretty good about ourselves. We can keep it all together. There's only one problem. Our old pride has taken over again—and we don't need Jesus any more. Our hearts are stone-hard again.

Let's say that as a new Christian you got irritated with someone and yelled at them. You'd feel so terrible that you'd confess it to God immediately: "I blew it. I just ripped Joe to shreds." You'd feel bad about the situation, so you'd make it right.

But slowly you get sophisticated. When you get mad at Joe, no one except you knows it. You don't yell at him anymore—you just avoid him. You make snide comments to other people about what a rotten job Joe is doing. A little slur here, a little gossip there. But you're not mad at Joe. Heavens, no. That wouldn't be Christian.

You can fool yourself. You can fool others. But you can't fool God.

Do you find yourself going through the motions? Using all the right clichés, all the Christian expressions? You know the right tone of voice and how to keep a smile on your face. You can smell like a rose on the outside—but inside it's a garbage heap.

I know this is true, because I fall into this sin myself. It's easy to do.

If you keep up the false front, the rot only continues. Before long, you give up on being a lover of God. You lose the intimacy with Him. You say to yourself, "Who needs the Spirit? Let's finish in the flesh."

No one deliberately sets out to go off the path. But the truth is, living the deeper Christian life with Jesus takes more time, more effort, more breaking of our will to continue in the Spirit than we're willing to give. It takes our all. So we come up with a "good idea." Wouldn't it be easier on our flesh to keep a list of rules?

Paul warned the Galatians:

> You foolish Galatians, who has bewitched you, before whose eyes Jesus Christ was publicly portrayed as crucified? This is the only thing I want to find out from you: did you receive the Spirit by the works of the Law, or by hearing with faith? Are you so foolish? Having begun by the Spirit, are you now being perfected in the flesh? (Galatians 3:1-3).

Paul was writing to a group of converted Jews—that's why he asked them if they received the Spirit by works of the law or by faith. As their faith and their first love for the Lord petered out, they fell back into what was familiar to them—legalism. They started to worry again about circumcision and about keeping a list of rules.

Now you and I don't do exactly the same thing. When our walk with the Lord gets dry and dead, we don't think about whether we should be eating kosher foods and sacrificing bulls again—we never did that in the first place. But we have our own set of dead works we fall back on.

I start to walk by sight again—I rely on logic instead of listening for God's leading. And I start reacting to people and situations the way I used to before I was a Christian. It's a subtle shift. It's a sign that my love relationship with the Lord is dying. I become dependent on my reasoning and not on my relationship with God.

Have you ever had someone make a major decision for you without consulting you? I've had people say to me, "Well, Keith, I told so-and-so that you would do this, because I know that's what you would want to do." I raise my eyebrows. And they go, "Well, umm. I've known you for two months and you always do it that way. I just thought that's the way you'd do it again."

No one can make a commitment for you without asking you first, isn't that right?

So how do you think God feels when Christians do that to Him every day? They say, "God would want me to teach the Bible this way." Or, "From what I know of God, I'm positive He'd want me to take this job." We may guess right some of the time, but God doesn't want us to second-guess Him on His will for our lives.

Where *is* God while these decisions are being made for Him? Is He out of touch? Inaccessible? Is He deaf? Here's the sad part: *His Spirit is right inside us.* He can't get any closer to us than that. God has made hav-

---

You have enjoyed yourself in Christianity enough. You have had pleasant feelings, pleasant songs, pleasant meetings...much happiness and handclapping and shouting of praises. Now then, to go down among the perishing crowds is your duty...your crown is in helping them to bear their cross...

— William Booth

---

ing a relationship with Him as convenient for us as possible. And yet we let our love for Him go cold.

Whenever I think I've got God figured out, He does things in a way I haven't seen before. He does that to get my attention. To keep me dependent on Him, and not on my "spiritual knowledge." God doesn't want me to depend on my so-called knowledge. He wants me to depend on Him. That doesn't mean that God is constantly changing or evolving so that I can't know Him. No. It's just that He's so great that I continually find new sides to Him. This *ancient newness* of God is a paradox.

> "For My thoughts are not your thoughts, neither are your ways My ways," declares the Lord. "For as the heavens are higher than the earth, so are My ways higher than your ways, and My thoughts than your thoughts" (Isaiah 55:8-9).

I wonder if God gets tired of our trying to interpret His actions. Imagine an ant trying to figure out human beings. The ant sees us do something one way once and makes a religion out of it. He becomes an expert on us. "Oh yes," he tells the other ants, "that woman will come out of that building when the sun goes down. She'll get in that thing with wheels on and it will take her away." So one day we go outside at noon to get the mail, and ruin the ant's theology. He feels like we've failed him. We didn't do things his way. All the other ants respected him as the authority on human beings, and we've made a fool of him.

How often do we do this to God? We try to tame him and fit him into the box of our expectations and understanding. But God is not a tame God. He can't be tamed by humans, like a lion at the circus. God is not domesticated. He's not figure-out-able. He cannot be cornered. He is not a formula. God is not bound by any rules. Some people say that God is bound by His Word. His Word is bound by Him. He doesn't read our theology books and say to himself, "Okay, I see that I'm allowed to do *this*—but I had better not do *that*, because they don't think I would." God is totally free. He's not required to submit to anyone.

He is the Creator—of everything physical *and* spiritual.

To fear the Lord means that we never usurp God's role. We never take His place in deciding when, where or how He's going to act. True, we can always know that His motives are love, mercy, bringing people to repentance and so on. But we can never know *how* God is going to do something. We can't depend on any particular pattern of how God will do things. We can depend on Him to love us—but we can't predict how He'll demonstrate that love to us.

So we can trust God's *character*. But we can also expect that He'll deal with us differently from our neighbor. He may deal with them with patience and gentleness. Then we expect the same from the Lord. But He comes down hard on us, and we say, "Wait a minute God. What about that guy? You were gentle with him." And the Lord says, "What is that to you? I am his God, and I am your God. I will treat you justly, but my justice is only understandable to me. Don't try to figure me out, because I work differently in different people's lives. But I'm working to the same end. I'm just going to get there in different ways."

Do you see why each one of us needs to stay fresh and warm in our relationship with the Lord?

In the flesh we're always trying to reduce *relationship* to *rules*. Jesus spoke to the chief religious leaders of His day:

> "Truly I say to you that the tax-gatherers and harlots will get into the kingdom of God before you" (Matthew 21:31).

His message to those of us who love the Word of God is this: "You know God's Word and all its requirements. You know all the prophecies—every shade of meaning and every possible interpretation. But be careful—because you may not know *Me*. I came to fulfill the law. If you get stuck on rules and don't know Me, then the most rotten sinner has more chance of getting into heaven than you do."

The Pharisees were an interesting group. They loved to walk around in public with long tassels on their robes and with long beards. They prayed longer, louder and more publicly than anybody else. They had more rules and regulations than the Marine Corps. Today, we laugh at them. Everyone but them could see how pompous and ridiculous they looked. In fact, they were the only group of people that Jesus got angry at. He had time for lepers, the Samaritans, the tax collectors and the prostitutes. But what did He say about the Pharisees?

> "Woe to you, scribes and Pharisees, hypocrites! For you tithe mint and dill and cummin, and have neglected the weightier provisions of the law: justice and mercy and faithfulness; but these are the things you should have done without neglecting the others. You blind guides, who strain out a gnat and swallow a camel!...For you clean the outside of the cup and of the dish, but inside they are full of robbery and self-indulgence" (Matthew 23:23-25).

Picture it. These pompous, religious people are out in their gardens, crawling around on the ground counting leaves on their herb bushes. They use their loudest voices to count, so everyone will know how holy they are as they pick every tenth leaf to tithe to the Lord. Forget about not letting your left hand know what your right hand is doing—these guys let the whole neighborhood know.

It's funny to think of the Pharisees doing these things, but we're all candidates for becoming as cold-hearted as they. All we have to do is love the Word of God more than God. All we have to do is love written truth more than living truth. All we have to do is to want to spend more time pursuing knowledge than the One who gives knowledge. All we have to do is try to defend religion rather than the Giver of true religion. All we have to do is love our blow-out prayer and praise services more than the One who is high and lifted up.

Here's a warning: As true relationship with the Lord becomes less of a priority to us, we learn how to imitate the Spirit. We learn to imitate spirituality. Someone once said to me, "If the Holy Spirit left all the churches in America, ninety percent of the church members wouldn't even know He had gone."

If the Holy Spirit left you, how long would it be before you noticed? That was Jesus' complaint about the church at Ephesus. He said to them, "You and I both know all the great things you're doing. But look, guys— I'm not there with you anymore. Did any of you happen to notice I was gone?"

There's only one thing God did not have before He created us— friends. There was nobody to be His friend. So He created us to share His heart, His thoughts and His joy. God longs for friendship, fellowship and relationship with us. Even when we blew it, He had a plan to restore fellowship with us.

> "For this is the covenant that I will make with the house of Israel after those days, says the Lord: I will put My laws into their minds, and I will write them upon their hearts. And I will be their God, and they shall be My people. And they shall not teach everyone his fellow citizen, and everyone his brother, saying, 'Know the Lord,' for all shall know Me, from the least to the greatest of them" (Hebrews 8:10-11).

There was supposed to come a time when all God's people knew Him for themselves—from the most important leader to the most insignificant follower. I can hear God cheering! At last people would really know Him. Old people, young people, fat people, skinny people. People could know God personally instead of relying upon other people to tell them about Him.

Jesus announced that the new covenant—this new way of knowing God—had come at last.

> "No longer do I call you slaves, for the slave does not know what his master is doing; but I have called you friends, for all things that I have heard from My Father I have made known to you" (John 15:15).

What do we do with the friendship of God? What do we do with His desire for intimacy with us? Are we prepared to be called friends of God? Are we the ones who will fulfill the longing in His heart? Or will He have this charge against us—"You are going through all the spiritual motions like an expert, but you've lost your first love. You've let your love relationship become an empty form. You started in the Spirit—and ended in the flesh."

Ask God now—cry out to Him: "God, set my heart on fire with real love for you!" Commit yourself to becoming a friend of God.

Don't let another day go by—not one more minute.

May the Lord himself say to you, "You started in the Spirit and you have *finished* in the Spirit. Well done, my friend."

Let this be the testimony of each one of us on that day when we stand before Him.

Jesus said,

"If anyone

    wishes to come

  after Me,

let him deny himself,

    and take up

      his cross,

  and follow Me."

Mark 8:34

Proclaim Him Lord

"Why do you call Me, 'Lord, Lord,' and do not do what I say?" (Luke 6:46).

"Well done, good and faithful slave...enter into the joy of your master" (Matthew 25:21).

◆

Being one of Jesus' first disciples couldn't have been easy. He continually challenged their motives for doing things. One of the toughest questions He ever posed was this one in Luke 6: "Why do you call Me, 'Lord, Lord,' and do not do what I say?"

Jesus holds out the same challenge for us.

He throws out this challenge to us because He knows how our human nature works. He knows that we want the security of friendship with Him. He knows that we want His love and peace in our life. That we want to know we're going to spend eternity with Him. But He also knows that in our human nature we don't want it to cost us anything. We want something for nothing from Him. We want a one-way friendship with Jesus. We want to be in His personal "bless-me club."

But that is not how Jesus sees things. His challenge brings us face-to-face with one of the great paradoxes of the gospel. Yes, salvation is God's free gift to us. But receiving that gift is going to cost us everything—our very life. To receive God's gift we must surrender our life to Him, die to our old self and be born anew into His family. And that was what Jesus challenged His disciples with, and what He challenges us with. Have you truly died to yourself? Who is ruling on the throne of your life? Are you still in command, or is Jesus? Are you saying you are one thing and then living as though you're something else? Jesus asks, "Why do you call Me, 'Lord, Lord,' and do not do what I say?"

To further drive home His point, following His challenge, Jesus tells us about a wise man and a foolish man. The two men built houses. The wise man dug down deep until he hit rock and built the foundations for his house on that rock. The foolish man, though, wanted to get on with building his house, so he built right on top of the sandy soil, and didn't worry about a deep foundation.

Now if you build a house without worrying about the foundation, you're going to be finished building a long time before everyone else. In fact, you're going to look pretty smart to passersby as you relax on your balcony and watch others doing their building. People will probably think, "This guy's smart. Look at the house he's built with a minimum of effort."

Those same passersby will see one who is laying a foundation on rock and say to themselves, "That's crazy! So much slog, so much sweat and effort for a house that looks just like the other guy's house, and it's already finished."

But then a storm comes. There's a flood, and it washes away the house that is not built on a proper foundation. The house on the solid foundation, though, stands firm. Now who's the crazy one?

In our walk of faith, we are continually tempted to build our spiritual houses on sandy soil. Foundations aren't that pretty, they aren't showy. People don't go by and say, "I just love your foundation." Foundations usually aren't noticed. And human nature wants to skip over the foundation altogether and go straight to the things people are going to see. The spectacular things. The public, high-profile things.

If a pastor asks for someone to lead worship, he is flooded with volunteers. But if he asks for volunteers to clean the church bathrooms or work in the nursery, where are all the volunteers? Somehow we can manage to find enough time to prepare for worship, but not enough time to help with a practical thing like cleaning a bathroom. Why? We all know the answer. Where's the fame? Where's the glamour? Where's the reward in cleaning a toilet for Jesus?

In our flesh we would rather seek the praises of people than of God. We want to put on an outward show. That's what's important. Why worry about a foundation of inner obedience and servanthood to the

Lord? But worry we must, because Jesus pointed out that if we don't resist the temptation to build upward before laying a solid foundation, then we will be swept away. Some storm of life will leave us in ruins. Everyone will see that what we did, no matter how impressive it looked at the time, was not built on a proper foundation in our life.

We cannot afford to attempt anything in the name of Jesus unless we're prepared to lay a solid foundation first. Just like a man who starts to build a tower without counting his money to see if he has enough to finish it (Luke 14:28-30), or like the five foolish virgins who didn't take enough oil with them to make it until the bridegroom came (Matthew 25:1-13), we dare not start something in the name of the Lord without digging down deep before we build up. If we do, we're doomed to fail.

But why did Jesus put these two things together? What do foundations and lordship have to do with each other? Jesus puts the two together because His lordship over every aspect of our life is the fundamental foundation God wants in our hearts. The New Testament always talks about making Jesus Lord, not simply Savior. So when Jesus gave the illustration of the two ways to build houses, He presupposed that those who invite Him into their lives are also going to make Him Lord. He wanted to point out how ludicrous it would be not to do that. "The ruin would be great," He tells us.

Recently a man came to visit our ministry and I asked him, "Are you a Christian?"

"Well, kind of. I'm what you call a backslidden Christian," he replied.

"But that's worse than being an outright sinner," I told him.

"I don't think it's that bad. I'm not immoral or anything. I still believe in God. It's just that there are some things I'm not ready to give up yet," he said.

He approached being a Christian as if he were buying a new car. When you buy a new car, you go to the dealership to check out the option packages. There are cloth seats and a fancy stereo with option one. Leather seats and a four-speed transmission with option two, and so on. When we become a Christian we check out the options. There's the Savior-only option. The lordship option. And the backslidden option. "Ah, that's the option I want, the backslidden option. That lets me do everything I want to do and still call myself a Christian. Then if I like the ride, I can trade up to the Savior-option or lordship-option package later."

This approach is simply an excuse for sin and compromise. It's an excuse for not making Jesus Lord of our life. It's a slight-of-hand trick so we can be called Christian without having to worry about the Christian-living part. But God isn't fooled by it. You can't trick your way into heaven. What makes us Christian is not our name, but our actions. Are our actions a mirror of Christ's actions? Do they clearly demonstrate His lordship over our lives?

If this is not the case with you, then what I told this backslidden Christian also holds true for you: "God is going to judge the world and everything in it. If you're holding on to anything when He comes to judge and destroy sin, then He's going to judge you and the loss could be very great."

> "Not everyone who says to Me, 'Lord, Lord,' will enter the kingdom of heaven; but he who does the will of My Father who is in heaven" (Matthew 7:21).

You can't get to the final judgement and *then* start calling Jesus *Lord* and hope to get into heaven. Lordship is something that is worked out here on earth.

But before we look at how we make Jesus Lord, we need to see what it is we mean when we talk about lordship. To make Jesus Lord of our life means to surrender control of every area of our life to Him. We come under His authority. His authority is supreme over our authority. We start taking orders from Him—we do what He tells us to do. That's what lordship is—Christ reigning as supreme authority over our life.

Making Jesus Lord of our life is not something passive. It's not a state of *being*, it's a state of *doing*. Those whom Jesus recognizes as His own are those who do the will of His Father in heaven.

When we read the Bible, there is no way we can get away from the call to *do*. Doing is the outworking of lordship—doing what He commands us to do. And by doing, we prove to all that Christ—not us—sits on the throne of authority in our life.

But the word *do* has been neglected by Christians today. We love to read the New Testament and note words like *blessed, receive, gift, promise, reward*. But not many like to note the word *do. Do* sounds like work. *Do* sounds like commitment. *Do* sounds like having to make difficult choices.

But Jesus' words challenge us: "Why do you call me 'Lord, Lord,' and don't do what I say?"

The world passes by the Church and laughs at how ineffective we've become. We're too stuffy, too selfish to get out and do what Jesus clearly told us to do. This in turn means only this: the Church no longer takes seriously Christ's claim of lordship over the lives of Christians.

But as Christians, we are called to action:

> But prove yourselves doers of the word, and not merely hearers who delude themselves. For if anyone is a hearer of the word and not a doer, he is like a man who looks at his natural face in a mirror; for once he has looked at himself and gone away, he has immediately forgotten what kind of person he was. But one who looks intently at the perfect law, the law of liberty, and abides by it, not having become a forgetful hearer but an effectual doer, this man shall be blessed in what he does" (James 1:22-25).

How do we become a doer of the word? By being sensitive to the voice of the Lord when He speaks to us, and by doing exactly what He tells us to do.

One time as Melody and I were flying back from a concert, I led the guy sitting next to me on the plane to the Lord. After we landed he went and flushed his drugs down the toilet, and then he looked at me and asked, "Now what do I do?"

Good question. What was I going to do? Was I going to say to him, "Well, praise God. Here's a tract, and here's the phone number of the church office. The office is open from nine to five, Monday through Friday. If you run into any difficulties, call them. Good luck, and praise God." I couldn't say that. I couldn't send him back to stay at the drug house he'd been living in. He needed a fresh start. He needed fellowship. He needed discipleship.

I knew the written Word of God, and as I pondered it I heard the Lord whisper, "If a man needs food, feed him. If he needs clothes, clothe him. If you have done it to the least—or the newest—of my brethren you have done it to me." I knew the Lord wanted me to invite this new Christian to come stay with us so we could help him get established in his relationship with God.

My flesh wasn't happy about what was happening. It wanted to get back on the throne and exercise a little authority. So it screamed at me, "Where will he sleep? Do you want to take financial responsibility for him until he gets a job? What if he won't get a job? Besides, you have enough to do. God is using you in other, important ways. You don't want to get bogged down ministering to a guy you met on an airplane."

But God had spoken, I knew what to do and soon we were on our way home with this newly converted guy riding along in the back seat.

It doesn't make any sense to be a Christian and not be Christian—to call Him Lord but not do what He says. That would be like saying to my wife, "I know I'm your husband, I have a certificate to prove it. But I can't live with you. I can't take care of you. I can't spend time with you. I can't sleep with you. But praise God for our commitment to each other. Praise God for our marriage."

Saying you're a Christian when you aren't willing to open your home, or aren't willing to sacrifice your time, energy, money and possessions is like saying to God, "I know You're my Lord. But I can't act like You're my Lord. I can't do the things You want me to do. I can't sacrifice the things You have commanded me to sacrifice. But bless Your name, You're my Lord." Saying that to God may seem crazy, but all too many of us say it to Him—and live it out in our actions.

I was like that. I was like the foolish man that Jesus talked about. I hadn't paid proper attention to the foundations of my relationship with Him. So God had to deal with me on the whole issue of lordship. One day I became conscious of Him speaking into my heart. He said, "Keith, why do you call me, 'Lord, Lord,' but don't do what I've asked you to? There are people in your neighborhood who you haven't even talked to."

"Well, I haven't felt you leading me to talk to them," I answered the Lord.

Then He gave me an interesting reply, one I wasn't ready for. "What's all this about 'feeling led,' Keith? Where did you get that idea from? Doesn't my Word say, 'Go into all the world and preach the gospel to every creature.' You haven't done what I clearly told you to do."

"But Lord, I've got to be realistic about things," I began reasoning. "I can't do all that right now. I have my family to take care of, and if I don't get enough sleep and relaxation my whole ministry will suffer."

Then the Lord said to me, "It's not your ministry, Keith, it's Mine. I gave it to you to be a steward over. I don't want you to win the whole world to me. All I want you to do is what you can. But you're not doing that yet. You keep usurping the authority you gave to Me. You don't do what I command."

When I heard these words from the Lord, I broke down and wept. He was right. I was good at calling Him Lord, but I wasn't really obeying Him.

A girl wrote me a poem recently. One of the lines said, "It isn't the ship in the water that sinks the ship, it's the water in the ship that sinks it."

It isn't the Christian in the world that creates problems, it's the world in the Christian that does. Our willingness to compromise Christ's lordship over us, sinks us. But if we believe the Word of God is true, we have no excuse. We have no other choice but to make Jesus Lord of our lives. We have no other option but to take seriously the things He has clearly commanded us to do.

But across the nation, many Christians are asleep. They've been lulled by the message delivered from many pulpits. A message that says we're doing fine. That the Lord is pleased with us. That all we need to do is hold on, because Jesus is coming back for us soon.

For a while I was lulled by this message. Until I read in Revelation the letters to the seven churches and thought about the situation. These seven churches seemed to have things together a whole lot better than I did, but God took a tough stand against them. So how come the only message I was hearing was that God was pleased with me?

Will you walk the path of repentance, and holiness, and zeal, and persevere until you are thoroughly awake in spirit?

— *Charles Finney*

I didn't have to wait long for an answer; the Lord spoke directly to my heart: "Keith, you're not listening to the right message. You're listening to the bless-me gospel. I want to mold your life after me, not modern Christianity. I want to be your Lord. But you must surrender that place of authority to Me. I won't take it by force. I want your willing submission and obedience."

We need to take seriously the lordship of Christ over our lives. The Bible teaches that either we submit to His lordship and allow Him to break us and transform our lives into His image, or we will eventually be crushed and destroyed through our lack of obedience.

> "And he who falls on this stone will be broken to pieces; but on whomever it falls, it will scatter him like dust" (Matthew 21:44).

This verse challenges us to be broken before the Lord. Every talent, every opportunity, everything we have must be surrendered to Him. It's not wrong to go to college. It's not wrong to get married. It's not wrong to own a house or a business. But all of these things need to be laid before Jesus. Like the loaves and fishes at the feeding of the five thousand, they need to be blessed and broken by God. Unless that happens, they serve no purpose but to distract us from serving the Lord.

Jesus fed five thousand people with a few loaves of bread and two fish. If we will give all of ourselves to Him, think of what He could do with us.

But too often we don't want to give all. We want to hold some back, in case things don't work out. We want to keep a little authority over our life, just to be sure.

I heard a story once about a beggar in India. This man had been begging all day long and had only a half-cup of rice to show for it. As he was rolling up his begging mat and preparing to leave, he heard the sound of the army approaching. The prince was coming! So he sat down again and waited for the prince to pass by. But as the prince approached, he stopped, climbed down from his elephant, went over to the beggar and asked him for some of his rice.

The beggar stared at him. "What nerve," he thought. "The prince wants my rice. He can afford to buy sacks of rice, and he wants me to give him mine."

Not wanting to refuse the prince, but also not wanting to give up too much of his rice, the beggar counted out three grains and handed them over.

Graciously the prince took the grains of rice and showed them to his head servant. As the prince moved on, the head servant walked over and dropped three gold coins in the beggar's lap. When he saw the coins he ran after the procession, offering the rest of the rice. But nobody took notice of him.

Of course, if the beggar had known he was going to get a gold coin for every grain of rice he gave, he would gladly have given it all.

The Prince of heaven wants us to exchange all that we cling to for immeasurable riches. Are we going to make the same mistake as this beggar and hold back?

People like my singing and piano playing. But when I came to the Lord, He asked me to lay it down. And I did, not knowing if He would ever let me play and sing again. But I'd have been a fool to cling to it. What's my talent compared to the one who fashioned the universe? What's my most creative thought compared to the creativity of the one who formed us from dust?

Why are we reluctant to hand our lives completely over to God? Why are we reluctant to give Him our bag of rice? Only a fool refuses to give God what He asks for.

God desires a people who will make Him Lord over their lives. Not in lip service but in reality—in what they do, not just in what they say.

If making Jesus Lord of our lives is not of utmost importance to us, then we're wasting our time and God's. In Revelation, Jesus says to the church at Laodicea,

> "I know your deeds, that you are neither cold nor hot; I would that you were cold or hot. So because you are lukewarm, and neither hot nor cold, I will spit you out of My mouth" (Revelation 3:15-16).

It's time we evaluated our commitment to Christ as Lord. Like the one who dug deep and laid a solid foundation before building, we must dig deep in our lives and lay a solid foundation of lordship.

Only a life totally committed to God can answer His challenge to us: "Why do you call me 'Lord, Lord,' and do not do what I say?"

Let's not be Christians merely in what we *say*, but in what we *do*. Let's be people who can say wholeheartedly, "Jesus is my Lord."

And if Jesus is not Lord of all, then He's not Lord at all. For such persons, their ruin will be great.

AFTERWORD

Some closing thoughts from Melody:

God wants to raise up a mighty army of Christian disciples in this generation—and He wants you to be one of them. You might be called to serve Him in your community or across the globe, but the mission is the same. He wants all of us to yield totally to Him so He can powerfully touch people through us.

I was convicted about some things after reading this book. Has the Lord spoken to you? If the Holy Spirit underscored some areas in your life, I want to encourage you to commit yourself to working them through with the Lord. Maybe there are things He wants you to change or adjust—or things He wants you to stop, or begin, doing. Whatever the case, don't put off the changes the Lord wants you to make. I've found that whenever I resist the Holy Spirit, I've only fallen further behind spiritually.

Of course, none of us who love the Lord would come right out and say, "Forget it, God. I'm not going to obey You." But our flesh is incredibly creative at inventing "spiritual" ways to put God off. Amazingly, we can rationalize, procrastinate or even counsel or "pray" ourselves right out of God's will. If we were half as creative at winning the world for Jesus as we are at finding ways to dodge His watchful eye, the world would probably be evangelized by now.

Each of us needs to line up our life with the revealed truth of God. Probably most of us have a list of priorities written down somewhere—a list given to us by the Lord after a time of prayer. The value of our list depends on how we use it. If we refer to it to make sure we're on track with God and occasionally revise it as He leads, it will be a helpful spiritual tool. But our list can also become a false sense of security if we say, "Lord, this is the intention of my heart," but don't make a genuine and consistent effort to accomplish those intentions. Then what we're really saying is "Here's my list God, but don't hold me to it."

Our list means nothing. How we live means everything.

Looking at how we spend the bulk of our time, talent and resources—financial and otherwise—reveals to us our priorities. When we stand before the Lord it will be useless to pull out our sheet of paper to show Him that He was at the top of our list.

God will judge us by our lives, not by our lists.

He is not looking for good intentions. He is looking for good fruit.

The parable of the sower, in Matthew 13, tells us those who are "good ground" (or genuinely saved) will yield fruit in different measures—thirtyfold, sixtyfold and a hundredfold. Some will bear more fruit than others, and enjoy a greater ministry, because they're willing to pay a greater price in obedience, sacrifice and spiritual discipline. There are many unfulfilled believers who covet the fruit they see in the lives of others. But we can't expect hundredfold results if we've only been living thirtyfold lives.

We need to be very honest with ourselves. Are we really the salt and light of the earth? Are we shining brightly like a city on a hill? Is our Christianity relevant? Do our neighbors and the people we work with know what we believe and why?

Someone once said, "Everybody wants to go to heaven, but nobody wants to die." We all want the benefits of God's promises, but we don't want to die to ourselves to get them. Then we wonder why our Christianity seems so blah. The problem is that we don't move from being babes in Christ to mature, fruit-bearing believers. We enthusiastically agree that Jesus means everything to us, but we don't live like it's true.

At one time or another, maybe after a convicting sermon, most of us have told the Lord, "All I have belongs to You—my home, my car, my money. If You ever want anything, just ask." This sounds great, but it puts the total responsibility on God *if* He ever wants anything, to interrupt our lives with a request. Instead, we need to view the possessions He's given us as tools to help others. Jesus doesn't care about our things per se, but how we use them indicates who's really in charge of our lives—us or Him.

The Scriptures tell us that all we have already belongs to God. When our doctor says, "Go home and go to bed," we don't wait for him to phone and say, "It's time to go to bed now." He has already given his instructions. So has the Lord, and He shouldn't have to repeat himself before we obey. We already know everything we have is His. It's our responsibility to ask Him how He wants us to use it to best fulfill His purposes on earth.

Of course, we know God loves us in spite of our weaknesses and shortcomings, but we can't forget that we're called to be obedient disciples who bear fruit. If something is really important to us, we'll make an effort to make it happen.

The Lord asks each of us to assess our lives to see if we're bearing fruit for His glory. If we've really made Jesus our Lord, our lives will be distinctively different from the lives of people in the world. Is your life different? Are you living the way Jesus wants you to live? The Holy Spirit can help you discern the truth. We can make powerful emotion-filled commitments to God, but when it comes down to the issue of who owns our time, our career, our leisure—we find out who is really in charge of our life.

It's time for all of us to go beyond the comfort zones of our family and church and look outward to see how we can be a greater witness for Christ. Maybe it's time to invite a neighbor or co-worker home for dinner to build a relationship that may lead to their salvation. Or, maybe it's time to take that missions trip the Lord has been speaking to you about. There are people dying every day who don't have a relationship with Jesus. We have the love and the answers they need.

If you are serious about making a difference in the world, you can. You can make a fresh commitment to the Lord today. Ask the Lord to show you anything in your life that grieves Him, then if He does, turn away from it. God is faithful to give you the strength you need to make any changes He's asking you to make. Then look for others who want to serve the Lord as strongly as you do. Find a group of believers in your church who will encourage you to keep growing and pressing forward. They might not be in your regular circle of friends, but look for those who have hearts for the Lord.

Let's let our love for Jesus grow until our greatest desire is to serve Him and tell others about Him. The Lord is looking for believers who will dedicate themselves to being wholly pleasing to Him—and go the extra mile with Him to impact this generation.

Today like never before we have opportunities to communicate the Gospel. Let's get going! Let's prepare our hearts and our lives to be filled to the brim with the love of God and the power of the Holy Spirit—and then go out and share His love with others.

Eternity will not be the same because of it.

What is LDM all about anyway...

Dear Brothers and Sisters in Christ,

Just as Keith's music ministry and teachings continue as an inheritance to this generation, so does Last Days Ministries (LDM) and its many areas of outreach. Last Days is an ongoing reflection of Keith's heart for the Lord and the world.

In 1977 when Keith and I founded LDM we were only a few years old in the Lord. How it came about is an incredible story and if you haven't read *No Compromise. The Life Story of Keith Green,* I hope you will. I think you'll be encouraged in your faith as I share how Keith and I became Christians and began a ministry in our home that ended up touching the world. We never dreamed the Lord would use LDM so powerfully!

When the Lord took Keith home in 1982 I continued on in leadership as the director of Last Days, and God has been faithful. One thing Keith and I prayed about finally came to pass in 1991 when LDM became a part of the international missions organization Youth With A Mission (YWAM). We also linked arms with YWAM's University of the Nations and now we're training others to communicate the Gospel in powerful, relevant ways.

In 1991 another important "linking" took place. Some dear friends who were very close to me and Keith introduced me to Andrew Sievright. Andrew came to the Lord in the late 60s and had been serving Him ever since. Along with sharing similar losses and life experiences, we found we shared a common vision for music ministry, reaching the lost, and a heart for equipping believers. After over a year of prayer, counsel, and falling deeply in love, we knew the Lord had called us to be married. Our wedding was in July of 1991. Because of Andrew's natural leadership and management giftings, and his vision and love for LDM, we've enjoyed serving God as a team. Today we are leading Last Days Ministries together – and things are really getting exciting!

The Lord is getting ready to pour out His Spirit in a fresh way and the enemy, knowing what's coming, has been attacking believers and unbelievers with a renewed vengeance. LDM has always been committed to win the lost and encourage the Church into action, so we're stepping up to this current spiritual challenge with determination. We're challenging Christians everywhere to hold up a godly standard through prayer, action, and living sold-out lives! In the last year alone we've sent LDM Ministry Teams to India, Nepal, Russia, Albania, Bulgaria, Romania, Haiti, Mexico, Israel, Brazil, Bolivia, Belize and throughout the U.S.A. Thousands have given their hearts to Christ as a result!

In the next few pages we'll tell you a little more about our vision and how you can get involved. We'd also love to send you the next four issues of our Last Days Magazine as a free gift so you can get to know us better – no strings attached! Just write with your request and mention reading about it in this book. May the Lord bless you as you serve Him with all your heart!

Melody

Last Days Ministries

Last Days Ministres

LDM is a community of believers committed to Jesus Christ and to each other. We're called to serve the Lord with all our hearts, first as individuals and then together as a ministry.

Our hearts burn with a passion to declare God's glory across the earth through prophetic and creative communications that challenge Christians to a deep devotion to Jesus Christ – and reach those who don't know Him with the message of His great salvation.

God has called LDM to train Christians to proclaim HIS TRUTH with excellence in dynamic, contemporary ways. Christians should be on the forefront of creativity and state-of-the-art technology!

The power of the printed page, spoken word, and song literally shapes the morals, culture, and mind-set of the world. We're teaching Christians how to use these skills with life-changing anointing and godly integrity.

But we're not *just* about training. We will continue to develop powerful ministry materials with high-quality visual impact and cutting-edge content.

COMMUNICATING Jesus IN

POWERFUL WAYS.

TRAINING OTHERS

TO DO THE SAME.

We want to see the Kingdom of God extended soul by soul – and *every* nation discipled in godly principles.

LDMers come in every size, shape, and color. We're from different nations and different church backgrounds – but we all have one desire.

We want our lives to make a difference.

International Communications Center • Youth With A Mission Base • Location: Garden Valley, Texas, USA • Approx. 200 Staff and Students • Full-scale Printshop • The Last Days Magazine (125,000 Subscribers) • Approx. 68 Million Teaching Tracts Printed So Far • Americans Against Abortion • LDM Music Ministry Teams • LDM Drama Team • Discipleship Training School • University of the Nations Campus: *Writer's Training School • School of Desktop Communication • *School of Video Production • *School of Music & Worship • School of Illustration • School of Print Production • *School of Theatre Arts

*Projected for spring and fall 1994
All statistics as of Summer 1993

Coming to you *in print*

Someone once said,
"The power of the press belongs to those who own one..."

We do.

It all started in 1978 in a little garage in Southern California.
We bought some used equipment and set out to change the world (or at least the Church) through our *Last Days Newsletter*.

We packed a whole lot of zeal and passion into those eight pages... and God used it. The tiny ripple became a wave, and that wave spread around the world.

If you're faithful with little, God will give you more.

He's given us a lot more. Today Last Days Ministries has a huge printshop facility. Our newsletter grew into the *LDM Magazine* and we've printed over 17 million of them, and 68 million discipleship tracts which have been translated by ourselves and others into 50 different languages!

LDM is preparing for the future. . .
and it's in communication.

Some of the stuff we produce in print:
Shown above from left to right: The Last Days Magazine • Ministry Materials
Catalogue • Teaching Tracts • No Compromise (biography of Keith Green) •
Christian Witness T-Shirts • Pro-Life Tracts and T-Shirts

Coming AT you   *music + videos*

It all started with Keith and Melody. The music they wrote, and Keith's anointed and passionate performance of that music, shouted a wake-up call to the Church.

And it's still shouting.

We are committed to communicate on-fire devotion to Jesus Christ with a whole new generation of believers. By sending out thousands of challenging audio and video teachings (taped and produced here at LDM) and producing the new music God has been giving us, we're staying on the cutting edge.

Our goal is simple.
We want to share the goodness of God ...
with the world.

Going to THEM   *ministry teams*

"You want to know my definition of a Christian?
Someone who's 'bananas for Jesus.'" **Keith Green**

LDM has always drawn people who are bananas for Jesus!

Our Ministry Teams have spoken to college students in Albania, led worship for Navajo teenagers in Arizona, distributed Bibles in the streets of Haiti, performed a puppet show in a Bulgarian orphanage, and taken evangelistic dramas into Russian scnools. You might even see us performing a drama or doing a worship concert at your church!

Our staff and students are single and married, young and young-at-heart, new converts and mature believers – but they all have one thing in common. They love Jesus, and they want to communicate that love to the ends of the earth.

God is a communicator. He speaks to us – and we speak to Him and to others about Him. Christians have incredible things to say! Unfortunately, few of us know *how* to say them. That's why, as part of Youth With A Mission, LDM has become an extension campus of their global university – the University of the Nations. Come to one of our schools and learn a lot more about God—and powerful ways of making Him known to others.

Discipleship Training: Let the Lord change your life in five incredible months. You'll learn about about God's character and principles as outstanding teachers share from His Word and their lives.Includes a six-week overseas outreach. A school for your heart, not just your mind.

*Desktop Communication: The pen is mightier than the sword, but next to the computer it's like a slow boat to China. Learn the latest advances in desktop publishing, graphics, photography, and video.

*Print Production: How to set up and maintain a small printshop – even if you have little or no knowledge of printing. An excellent skill for cross-cultural missions or any church or Christian organization.

*Three-month schools

*Illustration: Love to draw and paint? Learn to hear God's voice in the creative process as you develop your skills in watercolor, oils, sketching, and more! Taught by expert artists from around the world. A good picture is worth a thousand words!

†Music & Worship: Learn the keys to having the heart of a worshipper, which will make whatever style of Christian music you play life-changing for those who hear it. Also find out how to use your music to it's greatest potential. Learn from top Christian musicians and anointed worship leaders. One-week, one-month, and three-month schools.

*†Theatre Arts: Learn how to reach people in the power of the Spirit. Christian professionals in theater arts will instruct in areas including acting, mime, dance, improvisation, make-up and costuming. You'll learn how to perform on the stage or on street corners in evangelistic settings. We promise "dramatic" results!

*†Writer's Training: Love to communicate with words? Gifted Christian writers will show you how to create a scene, write dialogue, and "show" or "tell" situations. Learn how to use anecdotes and flashbacks, conduct effective interviews, and how to get your material published. Want to write articles or books? We'll help you become a powerful communicator.

For more information see "please send me stuff" page. For general inquiries please write or call:
Last Days Ministries, Box 40, Lindale, TX 75771, USA
Phone (903) 963-8671 FAX (903) 882-7709
9:00 am to 12:00 pm & 1:30 pm to 4:30 pm central time

†*Projected for spring and fall 1994*

our [HIS] tory

1975

Newly wed to Jesus and each other, Keith and Melody Green share the Gospel with anyone who will listen. In 1977, they officially begin Last Days Ministries.

1977

Keith's best-selling first album, "For Him Who Has Ears To Hear," sends a bold and powerful message to the Church. Many other albums will follow.

1979

Demand for back issues of the LDM Magazine led Last Days to reprint articles in tract form. The tracts have become an LDM "trademark" with over 65 million in print.

1980

The concert ministry of Keith Green continues to splash cold water on a sleeping Body of Christ!

1987

On behalf of LDM's pro-life arm, "Americans Against Abortion," Melody Green presents Ronald Reagan with a Petition For Life signed by almost three million Americans.

1991

Last Days joins forces with the missions organization Youth With A Mission. YWAM has over 400 bases operating around the world.

1977

Last Days Newsletter goes out as a prophetic voice to the Church. Today it's known as The Last Days Magazine and over 16 million have been sent around the world.

1979

Needing room to expand, the Greens and 23 others move their ministry base from Southern California to 140 acres in East Texas. LDM is now a place!

1981

The ranch undergoes a "building boom" – a cafeteria/worship center is built and a four-color Webb Press is added to the huge new printshop facility.

Keith Green, 11 Others, Killed in Plane Crash

The singer's evangelism and publishing ministries will continue, his wife says.

were his son, Josiah David, 3, daughter Bethany Grace, 2, ministry pilot Don Burmeister, 36, and the eight-member Smalley family.

John Smalley, his wife and six children, stopped at Last Days' 500-acre community on their way from California to Connecticut, where they were to begin a congregation. The Smalleys had known the Greens in California. Green's wife, Melody, and her...

"It was just going to be a ten minute tour of the

1982

On July 28th, Keith Green, with children Josiah (3) and Bethany (2), go to be with Jesus in an airplane crash. Melody, left with two children, is appointed director of LDM.

1991

Last Days celebrates the faithful love of God as Melody Green becomes the bride of Andrew Sievright on July 6, 1991.

1993

The LDM vision keeps expanding as we seek to obey the last command of Jesus – to share His message globally with a lost and hurting world.

Melody + Andrew...

Looking back it's amazing to see all God has done. But what He's doing now is just as incredible!

We're excited about the future because the Lord has promised that as we find fresh ways of sharing His powerful, life-changing message – with excellence – He'll open doors for it to go around the globe!

Our base is a constant buzz of activity as we continue to create new and relevant ministry materials to disciple believers and reach the lost. LDM Ministry Teams are going all over the world with people who love to worship the Lord and want to express it in a multitude of ways. But most importantly, they'll all have the fire of God to touch the hurting and lost. We desire to

see Christians encouraged in their giftings and shot like flaming arrows into the nations!

Although our outreaches include drama and music teams – the greatest need is for people with soft, willing hearts. People who will make themselves available to others by sharing the compassion of Jesus through the simple testimonies of what God has done for them.

We're really excited about our vision! If you are too, then maybe coming to one of our training schools is your next step – our personal invitation goes out to you!

Love in Jesus,

Andrew and Melody

come for training at LDM

please SEND me STUFF

For more information and free stuff, please fill out your name
and address. Check applicable boxes below and mail to:
Last Days Ministries, Box 40, Lindale, TX 75771, USA
(Don't want to tear out this coupon? Just photocopy it or write us and
request the materials or info – and tell us you read about them in this book!)

Print Your Name...

Address...

.... Zip ....

Telephone (   )..

❑ **Free Subscription to four issues of *The Last Days***
Magazine

❑ Free packet of our most
ordered message tracts
including messages by
Keith Green and Melody
Green Sievright.

❑ Free Ministry Materials Catalogue (*Mail-order list of available
Printed Materials, Music, and Videos*)

Send info on:

❑ Discipleship Training School

❑ School of Illustration

❑ School of Desktop Communication

❑ School of Print Production

❑ School of Theatre Arts

❑ Writer's Training School

❑ School of Music & Worship

❑ School of Video Production

GL01/B-C93

For information write or call:
Last Days Ministries, Box 40, Lindale, TX 75771, USA
Phone (903) 963-8671 FAX (903) 882-7709
Hours: 9:00 am to 12:00 pm & 1:30 pm to 4:30 pm central time